Joke, after Joke, after Joke, after Joke ...

Joke,
after Joke,
after Joke,
after Joke ...

by

Kevin Goldstein-Jackson

PAPERFRONTS

ELLIOT RIGHT WAY BOOKS
KINGSWOOD, SURREY, U.K.

Set, printed and bound in Great Britain by
Cox & Wyman Ltd, Reading

Contents

Dedication

Like all my books, JOKE after JOKE, after JOKE, after JOKE . . . is dedicated to the one I love (myself) and to all my friends who made suggestions for it – although my friends are far luckier than I am in that they can have *me* for a friend.

It is also dedicated to my mother-in-law for not being like any joke mothers-in-law in this book. (I have to say that, otherwise she'll beat me up.)

JOKE after JOKE etc. . . . . is also dedicated to Bruce (a kung-fu cat) without whom it would have been written in half the time; and (more seriously) to my mother as a token of my thanks to her for always sending on my post to wherever I happen to be in my frequent travels; and to Ng Mei Peng, SRN, for her help with jokes of a medical nature; and to Mei Leng – my most wonderful wife who always lets me have the last words in any argument: 'I apologize.'

Introduction

I'm writing this in my writer's room and have just been distracted by a tall lady walking past my window. I know she's tall because I'm on the seventeenth floor.

It's very difficult being a writer. Almost every day I get stopped in the street by girls who rush up to me and say: 'Hi, you gorgeous hunk of man – can you tell me the way to the nearest optician?'

I suppose writing jokes comes from my peculiar childhood. I was such a bad kid my parents ran away from home. And the area I lived in was so poor even the rainbow was in black and white.

In my teens I went crazy over one particular girl and for a long time we had a love-hate relationship – I loved her and she hated me!

Incidentally, I was told about the birds and bees very early in life. Shortly afterwards I was stung by a bee and was extremely worried for nine months.

It was difficult for me to get married. I had enormous problems finding someone who loved me as much as I did.

Perhaps it was partly due to being so 'dead' in the mornings that I can actually look into a mirror and spend half an hour wondering where I've seen that face before.

My life so far has been one brim-full of such small difficulties. Only this morning I was taking my usual bath in milk when the stupid cow slipped and fell on me.

But – enough of this rubbish! This is supposed to be an introduction to a book.

JOKE after JOKE ad infinitum ... contains over six hundred jokes listed alphabetically under assorted subjects. The Directory at the front gives a more detailed breakdown of the types and the suitability of the jokes.

Naturally, I don't claim to have written all the jokes in the book. Many have been told to me by friends; some you may have heard before – but then one can always say in reply to anyone commenting: 'That's an old joke' that 'So are your legs – but you're still using them.' Quite a lot of the jokes are my own, 'original' work – if it's possible to claim any jokes as being 'original'. Some of the jokes about secretaries and restaurants are not just jokes – the situations actually happened!

One point of particular note in this book: in the interests of equality I have included a section of 'husband' jokes which wives might like to use.

K.G-J.

Directory to the Book

If you are looking for a detailed breakdown of the sorts of jokes in this book, then here it is – if not, then skip the next few pages until the section labelled 'Jokes'.

The numbers given below refer to the number of the joke and *not* to the page number.

The jokes are listed by subject matter, with suggestions being made as to jokes which are especially quick to tell or suitable for particular occasions – like children's parties or for compères of various events and shows.

As a sufferer of many a boring speech, may I say please remember – if you're using this book to help with a speech – that the best speeches are like a well-kept lawn – short and neat?

And if any professional comedians are using this book, please think of me when you're rich and famous and drop cheques and twenty-pound notes through my letter-box.

13

587, 588, 589, 590, 591, 592, 593, 594, 595, 596, 597, 598, 599, 600, 601, 602, 603, 604, 605, 606, 607, 608, 609, 610
Writer: *Joke no.* 611

Zebras: *Joke no.* 362, 612
Zoo: *Joke no.* 591, 613

JOKES

A

ACTING
1. The Hollywood actress liked her tenth husband so much she decided to keep him for an extra fortnight.

ADVERTISEMENTS
2. Journalism – that extraordinary scribbling to be found in your daily paper, on the back of the advertisements. (With thanks to G. K. Chesterton.)

AMBIDEXTROUS
3. He'd give his right arm to be ambidextrous.

AMERICA
4. Shortly before the annual Independence Day celebrations of July 4th a nervous and inexperienced high school teacher in Evanston, Illinois, hands each child in her class a special book of facts all about their American heritage. She warns that she will be giving a stiff test just before the 4th. Anyone who fails will stay behind!

With the books all collected in on test day she fired question one: 'Who spoke the proclamation of the Second Continental Congress, declaring that henceforth the thirteen American colonies would become politically independent of Great Britain and then signed it and in which year?'

A subdued class said nothing. Then a hesitant voice ventured, 'Miss was it John Hancock in 1776?'

'Well done, Miguel! As for the rest of you, you should be ashamed; Miguel arrived here from Mexico only six weeks ago and *already* knows more than all of you.'

'Stuff the Mexicans!' a voice floated up from the back of the class.

'Who said that?' snapped the teacher.

'General Custer, at his last stand, battle of Bighorn, *1876*,' rejoined the voice, smugly.

5. A hillbilly boy from Nashville, Tennessee, announces to his folks: 'I's a'goin to Knoxville, to fetch me a wife.'

A few days later he returns with a nubile young sweetheart called Mary Lou. She is introduced to all the family, cramped around the kitchen table of their tiny shack.

Come six o'clock his father says, 'Well my boy, I guess you two deserve the family bedroom now. Your Maw and Paw can sleep down here.' So the happy couple go off upstairs. Half an hour later a shotgun blast rattles the timbers. And then the son clambers slowly down the steps from above.

'Whatever happened?' inquired his mother.

'I shot her,' said the son.

'Why?'

'She was a virgin.'

The boy's Grandpa, who had sat quietly through all these proceedings, was first to break the thunderstruck silence; 'Son, I guess you did the right thing – if she was no good to nobody in *her* family, then she ain't no use to any of us!'

ARMY

6. Two Army colonels were talking in the desert.

'I'm afraid Charles has gone a bit mad, old boy.'

'Oh! In what way?'

'He's run off with a camel, old boy. Actually eloped with the thing.'

'Was it a female camel?'

'Of course – there's nothing odd about Charles, you know.'

7. 'How long were you in the Army?'

'About six feet three and a half inches.'

ART CRITICS

8. Art Critic 1: 'I think the neo-Plasticism of the abtract design proves the mystical, metaphysical and non-humanistic approach to the objective concept of abstraction.'

Art Critic 2: 'Yes, you have a point there! In fact, it's obvious even from a casual glance that this painting was created by paranoiac-critical activity, brought about by spontaneous dynamic sensations, sometimes made by somnabulistically inclined campanologists, who create a picture of transcendental non-curvilinear and curvilinear objects expressing subjective feelings in a cubistic manner.'

Art Critic 3: 'I fully agree with you both – it's a rubbishy painting!'

AUSTRALIA

9. I went to Australia recently – but it was closed.

10. A man visited a large town in Australia and asked one of the locals: 'Does this town have any night life?'

'Yes,' replied the local, 'but she's ill today.'

B

BARBER

11. Barber: 'Sir, how would you like your hair cut?'
Customer: 'Off.'

BEAVER

12. The beaver said to the tree: 'It's good to gnaw you.'

BIBLICAL

13. Adam was the world's first book-keeper. He turned over a leaf and made an entry.

BIGAMY

14. The only thing that prevents me from being a big-amist is the thought of having two mothers-in-law.

BIRDS

15. The two birds met for the first time in a tree and one of them said: 'Bred any good rooks recently?'

BOOKS

16. The World's shortest book contained no words. Its title was: 'All I Know about Women'.

BOYFRIEND

17. My boyfriend has a good head for money – it's got a little slot in the top . . .

BUTCHER

18. The lady was searching for the last word in value in Christmas turkeys. The butcher showed her a bonny

bird but she hesitated and asked if he had a slightly bigger one.

'I will have a look in the cold store,' said the butcher, and disappeared for a minute or two.

In fact it was his last bird so what he did was to ruffle all the feathers up and put the bird into a shallow box so that it would look bigger.

'Here we are,' he said, 'is this all right?'

'Ooh, now that *is* super,' said the woman. 'I think I will take both!'

C

CANNIBALS

19. One tribe of cannibals were converted by missionaries to becoming good Catholics – they ate fishermen only on Fridays.

20. One clever cannibal toasted his mother-in-law at the wedding dinner.

21. The hippie cannibal ate three squares a day.

22. One cannibal wanted to become a detective so he could grill all his suspects.

CARS

23. The car was so old and dilapidated that someone scrawled on it: 'Rust in peace.'

CENTIPEDE

24. One day two male centipedes were standing in the street when a female centipede strolled past.

One male centipede turned to the other and said: 'Now, there goes a nice pair of legs, pair of legs, pair of legs, pair of legs, pair of legs . . .'

CHILDREN

25. The two little girls were busy boasting to each other about how great their respective fathers were.

'*My* father had lunch with Shakespeare yesterday,' said Sally.

'But Shakespeare is dead,' commented Clare.

'Oh,' replied Sally, unperturbed. 'No wonder dad said he was quiet.'

26. Angela's mother was looking in the mirror and plucking out the few grey hairs which she found in her head.

'Mummy, why do you have some grey hair?' inquired Angela.

'Probably because you're such a naughty girl and cause me so much worry.'

'Oh!' said Angela. 'You must have been a devil towards grandmother.'

27. 'Mummy,' said little Jimmy, 'I want to live with Carol next door.'

'But you're both only six years old,' smiled his mother. 'Where will you live?'

'In her bedroom.'

'What will you live off? You don't have any money – and what will you do if babies come along?'

'Well,' said Jimmy, seriously, 'we've been all right so far . . . and if she lays any eggs then I'll tread on them!'

28. A small boy was peering through a hole in the fence of a nudist colony. His friend, Paul, came up to him and asked: 'Tim, what can you see? Are they men or women in there?'

'I don't really know,' replied Tim, 'none of them have got any clothes on.'

29. Five-year-old Michael's mother was expecting another baby, so his father decided to have a little talk with him.

'Michael, something important is soon about to happen. A large stork will fly over the house carrying a bundle, and will drop the bundle down our chimney, and . . .'

'Oh!' interrupted Michael. 'I do hope the stork will

do it quietly and won't make a sudden noise and give Mum a shock; she's pregnant, you know.'

30. Five-year-old Steven: 'Are you a virgin?'
  Four-year-old Susan: 'No. Not yet.'

31. Little Fred came home from school after a particularly hard day and said to his mother: 'I wish I'd lived in olden days.'
  'Why?' asked his mother, curious to know the reason.
  'Because then I wouldn't have so much history to learn.'

32. Simon had been warned that he must be on his best behaviour when his wealthy aunt arrived for a brief holiday visit.
  It was at tea during the first day of her stay that Simon kept looking at his aunt then, when the meal was almost finished, he asked: 'Auntie, when are you going to do your trick?'
  'What trick is that, dear?' she inquired.
  'Well,' began Simon, 'Daddy says you can drink like a fish.'

33. Dorothy: 'Mum, did you know that Marconi was a famous inventor?'
  Mother: 'Yes, dear. But it's not polite to say Ma Coni – you should say Mrs. Coni.'

34. Mother: 'Where did all the jam tarts go? I only made them an hour ago and I told you not to eat them all – now there's only one left.'
  Fat son: 'So? I did what you said. I didn't eat them *all* – I left one.'

35. Tommy found the old, abandoned family Bible in the attic and opened it to find a large leaf pressed between its heavy pages.

'Oh,' he said. 'Adam must have left his clothes here.'

36. Samantha was a six year old who liked to exaggerate almost everything she saw or did.

One day she was looking out of the window when she called to her mother: 'Mummy, Mummy! Come quickly! There's a lion walking in the road outside our house!'

Samantha's mother looked out of the window, but could only see a small ginger cat.

'Samantha! You're lying again!' she scolded. 'Go upstairs to your room immediately and pray to God for forgiveness for being such a naughty little girl – and beg him to stop you from telling so many lies.'

Samantha ran up to her room, sobbing. A short time later she came down to her mother and said: 'I've prayed to God like you said, Mummy. And He said that *He*, too, thought the ginger cat looked rather like a lion.'

37. 'Mummy,' said little Desmond, 'at school today the religious teacher kept going on about "dust to dust and ashes to ashes". What did she mean?'

'I expect it means that we all come from dust and that, in the end, we'll return to dust.'

That evening, Desmond came running down the stairs from his room, calling anxiously for his mother.

'What is it? What's the matter?' she asked.

'Mummy! Come up quickly and look under my bed. Either someone has gone or someone is just coming!'

38. The little boy and girl were being bathed together and Sophie inquired of her brother, 'What is that?'

'That's mine,' said Hugo.

'Can I play with it?' questioned Sophie.

27

'No!' retorted Hugo – 'just because you've broken yours already!'

CHINESE
39. There is an ancient Chinese ceremony in which the parents of a child choose the baby's name.

As soon as the baby is born, all the cutlery in the house of its parents is thrown in the air. The parents then listen to the falling knives, forks, and spoons and choose a name: ping, chang, fan, fung, cheung . . .

CHURCH
40. It was Christmas morning and the family were plodding home from church through the snow, discussing the service. They all seemed to have a bad word to say.

Dad thought the bells had been rung dreadfully; Mum thought that the hymns were badly chosen; the eldest son fell asleep during the sermon and his twin sister could not agree with the prayers: all except for the youngest boy who opined; 'I don't know what you are all complaining about; *I* thought it was a damn good show for a penny!'

CINEMA
41. A young man was sitting in the cinema when a very fat lady got up during the interval and stepped painfully on his toes while squeezing past him into the aisle.

A short time later, the same fat lady returned, carrying an ice cream and a large packet of popcorn.

'Did I tread on your toes, young man?' she asked.

'I'm afraid you did. And you didn't apologize.'

'Good,' snapped the woman. 'Then this *is* my row.'

42. Just at the climax of an epic film an old man started grubbing around on the floor under the seats.

'What on earth are you doing?' the understandably irritated woman next to him rasped in a low voice.

'Trying to find my toffee,' said the man.

'Can't you leave it till the end? You are ruining the film,' snapped the woman.

'No!' croaked the old boy, 'It has got my false teeth stuck in it!'

CLEANERS
43. Office manager: 'Look at all the dust on this desk! It looks as if it hasn't been cleaned for a fortnight.'

Cleaning lady: 'Don't blame me, sir. I've only been here a week.'

CLOAKROOM ATTENDANT
44. Cloakroom attendant: 'Please leave your hat here, sir.'

Club customer: 'I don't have a hat.'

Cloakroom attendant: 'Then I'm sorry, sir, but you cannot come into the Club. I have orders that people cannot enter unless they leave their hat in the cloakroom.'

CLOCK
45. A young man purchased a large grandfather clock from an antique shop in Brighton.

He put the unwrapped clock over his shoulder and began to look for a taxi. He hailed one approaching from the right, but it ignored him so, swinging around, he tried to flag one down approaching from the left. Unfortunately, in turning around, the clock over his shoulder struck an old lady on the head and she fell into the gutter.

'Idiot!' she shrieked. 'Why can't you wear a normal wrist-watch like the rest of us?'

COMEDIAN
46. Comedian: 'Laughter is a wonderful thing – so other comics tell me!'

COMMITTEES
47. The difference between a good committeeman and a bad committeeman is that a good one sleeps upright and a bad one sleeps horizontally.

48. The last time I sat on a committee we were presented with a plan which had two alternatives. We therefore narrowed it down to eighteen possibilities for further discussion.

COMPÈRES
49. 'After such a warm reception I can hardly wait to hear myself speak.'

50. 'Now we have that fantastic lady singer who got to the top because her dresses didn't.'

51. 'Tonight, our pop group will sing a medley of their hit.'

52. 'There's always a long queue of people at his performances – trying to get out.'

53. Compère to heckler: 'Why don't you go and take a long walk off a short pier?'

54. 'We were going to have Morris Dancing – but Morris couldn't come.'

55. 'I see there's a very posh lady in the front row of the audience tonight. She's eating her chips with her gloves on.'

56. 'This evening, one of the beautiful chorus girls was hammering on my dressing-room door for more than fifty minutes . . . but I wouldn't let her out.'

57. 'He's just come from playing Julius Caesar. Caesar lost.'

58. 'Our next singer lacks only two things to get to the top: talent and ambition.'

59. 'Our next musician was even musical as a baby – he played on the linoleum.'

60. 'The last time he performed his act was right after the chimpanzees' tea party, and everyone thought it was an encore.'

61. 'The only thing wrong with the show tonight is that the seats face the stage.'

62. 'The next lady singer always wears dresses which seem to bring out the bust in her.'

63. Compère to heckler: 'There's a bus leaving after the show, sir – please be under it!'

64. 'Next we have a group who will make you want to stamp your feet . . . all over them.'

65. 'Our next guest is a politician who will be going straight to hospital after this show for a minor operation on his head . . . he's having a brain put in.'

66. 'Thank you for that amazing round of indifference.'

67. 'Our next singer is someone who wanted his name up in lights in every theatre in the world – so he changed his name to Exit.'

68. 'Our next comedian is so bad that when he took part in an open air show in the park twenty-three trees got up and walked out.'

69. 'Unfortunately, the actor who was to have been with us tonight has died. He caught a severe cold but, as you know, there's no curing an old ham.'

70. Compère to heckler who has just thrown a cabbage at him: 'I see a gentleman has just lost his head.'

71. 'Now I'd like to introduce someone who, ten years ago, was an unknown failure. Now he's a famous failure.'

72. 'The next act are currently riding on the crest of a slump and I'm sure you'll be completely underwhelmed by them.'

73. 'I see we've got a very polite audience here tonight – they cover their mouths when they yawn.'

74. 'Now we have someone who has been practising the violin for twenty years – it was only last week that he discovered that you don't blow it.'

75. 'Our next lady singer is wearing a very nice dress. I wonder when that style will be in fashion again.'

76. 'Our next act will probably be up to our usual substandard.'

77. 'When I was first starting in this business I was advised to make sure that my name was always the largest in lights outside the theatre – that way people knew it was a show to avoid.'

78. 'Now we have a six-piece band – they only know **six** pieces.'

79. 'Our next stripper is so awful, if she was a building she'd be condemned.'

80. 'The last time this singer was here he gave a very moving performance. Everyone moved out of the theatre.'

81. 'If my parents knew I was here tonight as compère they'd be ashamed – they think I'm in prison.'

82. 'Now we have a straight actress – she's 45-45-45.'

83. 'Now we have a rather portly trombonist. He could have been a violinist instead, if only he knew which chin to stick it under.'

84. 'Our next guest is that famous gossip columnist who, when she dies, will attract hundreds of thousands of people to her funeral – just to make quite sure she really *is* dead.'

85. 'Now we have a great puppeteer who broke into the business by pulling a few strings.'

86. 'The management have said I'm doing such a good job in this Club that they've decided to double my salary. Instead of getting ninety pounds a week I'll be getting it every two weeks.'

87. 'This is the last time I work as a compère at this Club. My dressing room is so small every time I stand up I hit my head on the chain.'

88. 'We close the show tonight with Samson – who is sure to bring the house down.'

89. 'Now we have someone whom success hasn't changed at all – he's still the rotten cad he always was!'

90. 'Our next singer once insured his voice for a million dollars. I wonder what he did with the money?'

CONFESSIONS

91. It was a regular coffee morning at Alice Gross-

white's house, and her two friends had got on to the subject of confessions and were detailing their secret vices.

'My trouble,' said Sheila, 'is that I'm such a flirt. I can't get enough of men and I've lost count how many times I've been unfaithful to John.'

'My problem is gambling,' commented Barbara. 'The housekeeping money soon runs out at the betting shop and I'm in debt up to my ears. But still the lure of the horses urges me on.'

'Hmm,' said Mrs. Grosswhite. 'My secret vice is probably worse than yours – I'm such a terrible gossip.'

CONTRACEPTION

92. A man went into a drugstore and bought a packet of contraceptives.

'That will be one dollar twenty cents – plus tax,' said the cashier.

'Don't bother with the tax,' said the man, 'I'll tie them on.'

CONVERSATIONS

93. 'Is it cold out?'
   'Is *what* cold out?

94. 'What do you think about bathing beauties?'
   'I don't know – I've never bathed any.'

95. 'Are you trying to make a fool out of me?'
   'Of course not! Why should I try to change Nature?'

96. 'Whatever I say goes.'
   'Please talk to yourself.'

97. 'What did you do before you got married to Gloria?'

'Anything I wanted to do.'

98. 'Are you a mechanic?'
'No. I'm a MacDonald.'

99. 'Excuse me, do you know how to pronounce "Hawaii"? Is it with a "v" sound or a "w"?'
'It's Havaii.'
'Thank you.'
'You're velcome.'

100. 'Which of your relations do you like best?'
'Sex.'

101. 'I went to the dentist this morning.'
'Does your tooth still hurt?'
'I don't know – the dentist kept it.'

102. 'My old uncle has one foot in the grate.'
'Don't you mean he's got one foot in the grave?'
'No. He wants to be cremated.'

103. 'Why did you push him under a steamroller?'
'Because I wanted a flat mate.'

104. 'Why are you drinking red and white paint?'
'Because I'm an interior decorator.'

105. Fred: 'I've just returned from a duck shoot.'
Tom: 'How was it?'
Fred: 'Terrible! All the others shot and I had to duck.'

106. Man in blood donor clinic: 'I've come to donate a pint of blood – where do I spit it out?'

107. 'Do you have holes in your trousers?'
'No.'
'Then how do you get your legs through?'

108. 'I'm trying.'
'Yes. You're very trying!'

109. 'Are you enjoying yourself?'
   'Yes, of course – what else is there to enjoy?'

110. 'Do you write with your left hand or your right hand?'
   'Neither – I write with a ballpoint pen.'

111. 'Why do you part your hair in the middle?
   'So that my head will be evenly balanced.'

112. 'Every Saturday and Sunday my father goes to the Old Folks Club. I don't know what exactly he does there – but he's got eight notches in his walking stick.'

113. 'Alison says she's been happily married for three years – which isn't bad, really, considering she's been married for thirty.'

114. 'You've never looked better in your life . . . whenever *that* was.'

115. Wife: 'Do you have a good memory for faces?'
   Husband: 'Yes. Why?'
   Wife: 'I've just broken your shaving mirror.'

116. 'Where's Ruth?'
   'She's abroad.'
   'I asked *where* she was, not *what* she was.'

117. 'What do you think of Red China?'
   'Will it clash with the purple tablecloth?'

118. Part of a 'phone conversation: 'Are you hanging up?'
   'No, I'm lying down.'

119. Overheard to a chauffeur: 'James, I'm now ninety and rather bored with life, so I want to commit suicide. Kindly drive over the next cliff.'

120. 'Are you going to take a bath?
   'No – I'm going to leave it where it is.'

121. 'I don't know what to do with my hands while I'm talking.'

'Why don't you hold them over your mouth?'

122. 'By the time we've paid for all the furniture we've just bought we shall be the proud owners of genuine antiques.'

123. 'Why are you jumping up and down?'

'Because I've just taken some medicine and I forgot to shake the bottle.'

124. 'I'm an atheist – thank God!'

125. 'Have you seen the duchess?'

'No – but I've seen an English "s".'

126. 'Get my broker.'

'Which one – stock or pawn?'

127. 'Why did you marry Sarah? Was it because her father is wealthy or is she pregnant?'

'Neither. I love her.'

'Oh. I thought there would be a catch in it.'

128. 'Three cheers for the flower people – hippy, hippy . . .'

129. 'There's a fish in my grand piano.'

'That's all right – it's only a piano tuna.'

130. 'Why are you putting starch in your vodka?'

'Because I want a nice stiff drink.'

COOKERY

131. 'I've made the chicken soup.'

'Good! I was worried it was for us.'

132. 'I've prepared the turkey,' said Charles proudly to his wife. 'I've plucked it and stuffed it. All you've got to do is kill it and cook it.'

37

133. 'Darling,' called the young bride from the kitchen. 'I'm afraid I've spoilt your breakfast. The eggs were frying nicely when all of a sudden the shells broke and it all became very messy.'

134. 'Quite honestly, Henrietta, I shall be glad when we've eaten the last of that rhinoceros . . .'

135. 'Urrgh!' said Mr. Blenkinsop, 'this lamb is tough.'
'I'm sorry,' replied his wife, 'but the butcher said it was a spring lamb.'
'Then that explains it,' said Mr. Blenkinsop. 'I must be eating one of the springs.'

136. Two students shared a flat and a cat. Neither of the students was a particularly good cook.
One day one of the students returned to find his flatmate wringing his hands in despair.
'What happened?' asked the student.
'The cat ate your dinner.'
'Don't worry,' replied the first student. 'We'll buy another cat tomorrow.'

COWBOY
137. 'Say! Aren't you the rotten, horrible, wicked outlaw who held up the Northwood Stage? How's your hernia?'

CRIMINALS
138. Joe Bloggs, a small-time jewel thief, came home after robbing a nearby country house and began to saw the legs off his bed. When his wife asked him what he was doing he replied that he wanted to 'lie low for a while'.

CUSTOMS

139. A customs officer at Kennedy Airport, New York, opened the suitcase of a beautiful young girl from England and discovered six pairs of very brief panties. He took them out of the case for further inspection (in the vain hope of finding some concealed drugs) and found that the panties were each labelled with one day of the week, from Monday to Saturday.

'And on Sunday?' he inquired.

The girl blushed.

The next person to be inspected by the customs officer was an enormously fat woman from Montreal, and the customs officer took out twelve pairs of giant-size bloomers from her suitcase. Before he could say anything, the Montreal lady smirked, patted his arm playfully and said: 'January, February, March, April, May . . .'

D

DEFINITIONS

140. Aperitif: a pair of French false teeth.

141. Minister of Defence: a man who is always ready to lay down *your* life for *his* country.

142. Polygon: a dead parrot.

143. Sandpaper: an Irishman's map of the desert.

144. Squawker: baby of a Red Indian squaw.

DESERT

145. The beautiful young girl had been kidnapped and then left, naked and abandoned and buried up to her neck in sand in the desert.

After crying for help for hours and hours until she was hoarse, her cries were eventually heard by a young film director who was searching the area for suitable locations for his next epic.

'Help me! Help me!' cried the girl.

'And if I help you,' said the man, 'what's in it for me?'

'Sand,' she replied.

DIETS

146. Mavis: 'My doctor put me on a new diet, using more corn and other vegetable oils.'

Beryl: 'Does it work?'

Mavis: 'Well, I'm not any thinner yet – but I don't squeak any more.'

DOCTOR

147. The man went to see his doctor because he was

feeling under the weather. The doctor asked the usual question such as had the man been drinking or eating too much.

'No,' said the man.

'Well, perhaps you have had too many late nights?' queried the doctor.

'No,' the man replied.

The doctor thought about the problem for a while and then asked 'much sex?'

'Infrequently,' came the reply.

'Is that two words or one?'

148. A woman went to her doctor to complain that her husband's sexual feelings for her seemed to have declined.

The doctor, being an old friend of the family, gave the woman some pills to slip into her husband's tea so that at least the man wouldn't get a complex about being a bit under-powered.

Two days later, the woman was back in the doctor's surgery.

'What happened?' asked the doctor. 'Did the pills work?'

'Fantastic!' replied the woman. 'I was so eager to see their effects on my husband that I tipped three of them into a cup of coffee and, within seconds of drinking it, he got up, kicked over the table and pulled me down on to the floor and ravished me.'

'Oh!' said the doctor. 'I hope you weren't too surprised.'

'Surprised?' said the woman. 'I'll never be able to set foot in that restaurant again . . .'

149. Handsome young doctor: 'Say "ah!" '

Pretty young girl: 'That's a change! Most young men want me to say "yes".'

150. 'Doctor, I wish to protest about the spare part surgery operation you did on me.'

'What's wrong? I gave you another hand when your own was smashed up at your factory.'

'I know. But you gave me a female hand which is very good most of the time – it's only that whenever I go to the toilet it doesn't want to let go.'

151. As the doctor said to his girlfriend: 'I love you with all my heart – and my kidneys, liver, epiglottis, spinal cord . . .'

152. The pretty nurse explained her problem to the doctor: 'Every time I take a man's pulse it goes up. What should I do?'

'Blindfold them,' replied the doctor.

153. 'Doctor, doctor! I keep thinking I'm a pair of curtains.'

'Well, pull yourself together.'

154. Mrs. Grunge: 'Doctor, it's about this bananas-only diet you've put me on.'

Doctor: 'What about it?'

Mrs. Grunge: 'It seems to be having rather a peculiar effect on me.'

Doctor: 'Oh, I wouldn't say that, Mrs. Grunge. Now, if you'll just stop scratching and come down from the curtains perhaps . . .'

155. After some months of marriage, a girl wrote the following letter to her doctor:
'Dear Doctor,
   Since I got married, my husband seems to have gone

mad. He is after me at breakfast, coffee break, lunch-time – even tea time – and then all night every few hours. Is there anything I can do or give to help him? I await your kind reply.

P.S.: Please excuse shaky handwriting.'

156. The doctor was visiting 78-year-old Jim at his home to give him a routine check-up.

'For a man of your age,' said the doctor, 'you're in excellent shape. How do you manage it?'

'Well,' replied Jim, 'I don't drink, I don't smoke and I've never played around with women and . . .'

He was interrupted by a crashing sound and female shrieks coming from the room immediately above them.

'What was that?' asked the doctor.

'Oh!' said Jim, 'only my father chasing the new au pair girl. He must be drunk again!'

157. Doctor, examining a patient: 'What's that strange growth on your neck?' (Pause) 'Oh – it's your head.'

158. Two doctors in the USA were talking.

1st doctor: 'Why did you perform that operation on Mrs. Weitzman?'

2nd doctor: 'Ten thousand dollars.'

1st doctor: 'No. Perhaps you didn't hear me correctly. What did Mrs. Weitzman have?'

2nd doctor: 'Ten thousand dollars.'

159. Mrs. Smith: 'Doctor, please can you help me? I've had twelve children and I'm pregnant again and I don't want any more kids after this one. I desperately need a hearing aid.'

Doctor: 'A hearing aid? What do you want a hearing aid for? Surely you want some birth control pills or some form of contraceptive device?'

Mrs. Smith: 'No, doctor. I definitely want a hearing aid. You see, my husband gets drunk every Friday night and comes lumbering into my bed and says to me: "Do you want to go to sleep or what?" Me being a bit deaf I always say: "What?" '

160. 'Doctor, is there something wrong with my heart?'

'I've given you a thorough examination and I can confidently say that your heart will last as long as you live.'

161. Doctor: 'Well, Mrs. Cuthbert, I haven't seen you for a long time.'

Mrs. Cuthbert: 'I know, doctor. But I've been ill.'

162. Worried young girl: 'Doctor, this new diet you've put me on makes me feel so passionate and sexy that I got carried away last night and bit off my boyfriend's right ear.'

Doctor: 'Don't worry, it's only about forty to fifty calories.'

163. 'Doctor, it's impossible for my wife to be pregnant. I'm a sailor and I've been away from her working on my ship overseas for more than a year.'

'I know. But it's what we call a "grudge pregnancy". Someone had it in for you.'

164. 'Doctor, doctor, I was playing my mouth-organ and I suddenly swallowed it.'

'Well, look on the bright side – you could have been playing a grand piano.'

165. Henry's doctor told him to be like a rabbit and eat lots of carrots to improve his eyesight, so he could see better at night in his work as a night watchman. His eyesight improved slightly, but he kept tripping over his ears.

166. Patient: 'Doctor, I've got diarrhoea.'

Doctor: 'Yes. It runs in your family.'

167. Doctor: 'Take three teaspoonsful of this medicine after each meal.'

Patient: 'But I've only got two teaspoons.'

168. Patient: 'Doctor, I keep thinking I'm a ball of string.'

Doctor: 'Well, go and get knotted.'

169. 'Doctor, I've got wind – can you give me anything for it?'

'How about a kite?'

170. Old man: 'Doctor, how do I stand?'

Doctor: 'That's what puzzles me.'

171. Doctor: 'Miss Smith, you have acute appendicitis.'

Miss Smith: 'I came here to be examined – not admired.'

172. It was three o'clock in the morning and the plumber's telephone rang. It was the doctor, saying that his toilet seemed to have broken and could the plumber come immediately to fix it.

The plumber reluctantly agreed to visit the doctor's house, although the plumber warned his client that at this time of night he could only expect him to provide 'a doctor's treatment'.

When he arrived, the plumber went straight to the offending toilet, threw an aspirin down it, and then said to the doctor: 'If it's not better by lunchtime tomorrow, 'phone me and I'll come again.'

DOGS

173. Fred: 'We've got a new dog. Would you like to come and play with him?'

Tom: 'I've heard him barking and growling. He sounds very fierce and unfriendly. Does he bite?'

Fred: 'That's what I want to find out.'

174. 'I washed my dog last night and he died.'

'Died? But why? Washing a dog can't kill it.'

'Well, it was either washing it or the spin dryer that did it.'

175. Timothy: 'I say, your dog is very clever being able to play the trombone.'

Algernon: 'Not really – he can't read a single note of music.'

176. Albert has got the laziest dog in the world. Even when he's watering his garden the dog refuses to lift a leg to help.

177. 'What is your dog's name?'

'I don't know. He refuses to tell me.'

DREAMS

178. Young man: 'Darling, I dreamt about you last night.'

Pretty young girl: 'Did you?'

Young man: 'No – you wouldn't let me!'

DRUNKS

179. It was a dark, cloudy night and the drunk staggered into the cemetery and fell into a hole which had been dug in preparation for a burial the following day. The drunk hiccuped and fell asleep.

Half an hour later another drunk swayed into the cemetery. He was singing loudly and his raucous voice woke up the drunk in the grave who suddenly started to yell that he was cold.

The singing drunk tottered to the edge of the grave and peered blurrily down at the complaining drunk. 'It's no wonder you're cold,' he shouted down to the drunk, 'you've kicked all the soil off yourself.'

E

EMPLOYERS

180. Boss: 'I don't like "yes" men. When I say "no" I want them to say "no" too.'

181. Our boss is so popular everybody wants to work for him – the local undertaker, the grave-digger . . .

182. The managing director of a large company – which he had founded – received a short job application letter for the position of assistant managing director from a young man who detailed his education at a top public school, outlined his aristocratic background and intentions of marrying the daughter of a duke – yet failed to give any indication of his competency or even knowledge of the job available.

The managing director therefore felt obliged to write back to the young man: 'Dear Sir, Thank you for applying for the position advertised. I am unable to employ you since we require the services of someone for managerial rather than breeding purposes.'

183. My employer is the sort of man who grows on you – like warts.

184. My boss is so mean that whenever he pays anyone a compliment he insists on a receipt.

185. 'Simpkins, how many people work in your office?'
'About half of them, sir.'

186. The new office boy was bitterly denying to his older colleague that he was a crawler: 'It's not true that I lick my boss's shoes every day – he's only in the office on Mondays and Thursdays.'

187. My boss thinks very highly of me. Today he even called me a perfect nonentity.

188. We don't know what to get our boss for Christmas. What do you get for someone who's had everybody?

189. The managing director looked around the board room after making his speech in favour of a particular course of action.

'Now,' he said, 'we'll take a vote on my recommendations. All those in opposition raise your right arm and say "I resign".'

190. You can't help admiring our boss. If you don't, you don't work here any more.

191. The only reason my boss never says an unkind remark about anyone is because he only ever talks about himself.

192. My boss is so unpopular even his own shadow refuses to follow him around.

EXAGGERATION
193. Mother to child: 'How many millions of times has your Father warned you *not* to exaggerate?'

F

FAIRY TALES
194. 'Mummy, why do fairy tales always start "Once Upon a Time"?'

'They don't always my dear. The ones your father tells usually start with "I got caught up at the office; sorry I'm late love ...".'

FAMILY TREE
195. One woman paid a genealogist five hundred pounds to trace her family tree – then she had to pay another five hundred to have it hushed up.

FARMERS
196. Farmer Jim was very worried about the poor performance of his prize bull for which he had paid an astronomical sum. He talked to all his friends every time he went to the market and one day learned from a cousin that there was an amazing vet way down in the West Country.

He was so depressed about the Bull that he decided this last resort was the answer and he took himself off to Cornwall to find the vet. At last he found the chap who urged him to give his bull a great big pill once a day.

A few months later he met his cousin who asked him how he had got on. 'Oh, it was marvellous,' he said, 'he gave me these pills for the bull and I had no sooner started him off on them than he hit the jackpot. In fact,' he said, 'I am making a fortune out of the local farmers – they can't get their cows round here fast enough!'

'What are these pills then?' asked his cousin.

'Oh!' said Farmer Jim, 'huge great green jobs like bombs, with a peppermint taste!'

197. Wealthy poultry farmer, Bernard Nurnberg, of Tucson, Arizona was over in the UK on a chicken safari, looking for new ways to boost his production. He arrived at a small farm near Ballachulish and announced himself to the diminutive Scots farmer, Hamish McTavish:

'The name's Nurnberg, Bernard Nurnberg,' he warbled, shaking the Scotsman's hand vigorously. 'I'm here to find out how you raise turkeys right here in Scotland. How large is your farm?'

'Och well,' said Hamish, 'if you look down the burn to your left that is my left-hand boundary. Where you see the woods in the distance is my bottom boundary. Now here on the right-hand side is a wee "tump", as we call it in Scotland (which just means a small hill) and if you look where we have burnt the heather in a long line along the side of the hill, that is my right-hand boundary. The roadway where you have just come in completes the square so really, when you are standing right here, you can see the lot.'

'Oh my,' drawled Bernard, 'compared to my estate in Arizona this is just a side-show! Why back home it takes three days just to drive my truck around the perimeter!'

'Is *that* so?' rejoined Hamish, and after a thoughtful pause, 'It will be some years now I suppose, since *I* had a truck like *that*!'

FILM CREDITS
198. Tents supplied by Marquee de Sade.

199. Lion tamer: Claude Bottom.

200. Costumes designed by Plaster of Paris.

FORTUNE TELLERS

201. A young girl visits a clairvoyant, who looking into her crystal ball, bursts out laughing. With a crack like a pistol shot, the girl slaps the medium hard across the jaw.

'*Ouch!* What was *that* for?' protests the fortune teller.

'My mother always insists that I should strike a happy medium!' the child explains.

FURNITURE

202. He bought a piece of antique furniture quite cheaply from a seafood restaurant. It was Fish and Chippendale.

G

GHOSTS

203. The father ghost told his son: 'Spook only when you are spoken to.'

204. Richard was not very frightened when he saw the ghost and, since it appeared to be friendly, he asked the ghost if he could try to photograph it.

The ghost willingly agreed and Richard went to fetch his camera, but found that the flash attachment on it was broken.

The spirit was willing – but the flash was weak.

205. Then there was the ghost who didn't believe in people.

206. Human: 'Do you plan to stay in this town very long?'

Ghost: 'No – I'm only passing through.'

207. The young ghost got very scared when his friends told him too many human stories.

GOLDFISH

208. 'Why haven't you changed the water in the goldfish bowl like I asked you to do?'

'Because they haven't drunk the first lot yet.'

GOSSIP

209. If you can't repeat gossip – what else can you do with it?

H

HAIRDRESSERS
210. A successful young 'Tycoon Designate' was enjoying the full works at a fancy hairdressing salon in the West End.

'Dressing, sir?' asked the barber.

'No, no!' came the swift reply. 'My wife might think I had been to a brothel.'

Unknown to him, his boss was also making an incognito visit to the high class establishment. When he was asked the same question he came out in fine voice for the benefit of his unsuspecting executive, who was still receiving a nail manicure, 'yes please, pile it on if you like. My wife has no idea of the smell you find in a brothel!'

HAIR STYLE
211. 'Do you like my new hair style?' cooed the trendy young girl to her somewhat conservative boyfriend.

'Well,' he said. 'It reminds me of a beautiful Italian dish.'

'An actress?' she inquired eagerly.

'No. Spaghetti.'

HAT
212. Charles used to wear a pork pie hat, but he got fed up with the gravy running down his neck.

HEAVEN
213. A Scotsman rapped angrily on the Pearly Gates after he had died.

'Who is it?' came a crisp voice.

'Jock McSporran; open up!' yelled the Scot.

'Sorry chum – we canna' begin making porridge for one in this hoose!'

HIPPIE

214. The hippie was being interviewed by a civil servant (known as a 'straight') and the conversation went something like this:

Straight: 'Why don't you wear proper clothes and cut your hair?'

Hippie: 'Why?'

Straight: 'If you smartened yourself up you could get a job.'

Hippie: 'Why?'

Straight (patiently): 'Because in a job you get paid money.'

Hippie: 'Why?'

Straight (getting a bit exasperated): 'So you can save some money.'

Hippie: 'Why?'

Straight (becoming extremely annoyed): 'It's obvious, you idiot! With the money you've saved you can retire and so not work any more.'

Hippie: 'I'm not working now.'

HOLIDAYS

215. The Chinese girl had just returned to Hong Kong from a holiday in England and was talking to her best friend.

'Mabel, I've been thinking about Keith ever since I left England. Now I'm back home I don't think I should write to him as our friendship was only slight.'

'But, Wendy, you promised to marry him!'
'I know. But that was all.'

216. 'Help, help!' shouted the man in the sea. 'I can't swim.'

'So what?' shouted back a drunk from the shore. 'I can't play the piano, but I'm not shouting about it.'

217. A beautiful young girl was lying, asleep, in a tiny bikini immediately below the promenade. A small boy accidentally dropped a piece of his vanilla ice-cream on her, and it landed on her navel.

The girl immediately awoke and sprang to her feet, shocked, and said: 'These seagulls must live in a flipping refrigerator.'

HONEYMOONS

218. 'Darling, just imagine – we've now been married for twenty-four hours.'

'Yes, dear, it's incredible. And it seems only as if it was yesterday.'

219. Cuthbert married a very refined virgin from an impeccable background, and took her away to Tunis for their honeymoon.

On the first night in their hotel, Cuthbert quickly stripped off all his clothes and jumped into bed and then watched while his wife slowly removed all her garments.

But Cuthbert was rather surprised when she clambered into bed completely naked except for her white gloves.

'Why don't you take your gloves off?' he asked.

'Because mummy said I might actually have to *touch* the beastly thing,' she replied.

220. It was in olden days and the bride and groom were setting off alone on their honeymoon – travelling by horse and carriage.

Suddenly, the horse reared up, startled by a snake in its path. Annoyed at the horse's behaviour, the man waved his finger threateningly at the horse and said: 'That's your first warning.'

They continued their journey until about half an hour later when the horse stopped at a water trough at the roadside to drink a few sips of water.

Again, the man was annoyed at this interruption in their journey, and he wagged his finger and said, menacingly: 'That's the second warning.'

They continued their journey until dusk, when again the horse reared up, rocking the carriage violently. The man clambered down from the carriage, took out his gun, and shot the horse dead between the eyes, saying as he did this: 'And that was the third time.'

The man's wife, on seeing this, burst into tears. 'What did you shoot the horse for? She was probably frightened by another snake or something similar. It wasn't her fault. Now you've killed her! How could you be so cruel! If I'd known you were such a sadist I'd never have married you! How could you do it to such a poor defenceless creature?'

As she began to cry uncontrollably, her husband wagged his finger at her and said: 'That's the first warning.'

221. The seventy-nine year old British knight had just married a sweet, innocent seventeen-year-old debutante.

'Tell me, my dear,' said the knight, 'did your mother explain to you the facts of life?'

'No, sir, I'm afraid she did not.'

'Oh, how awkward,' commented the knight. 'I seem to have forgotten them.'

222. As they lay in bed on the first day of their honeymoon, John turned to his wife and sighed: 'Darling, I hope you can put up with my ugly face for the rest of your life.'

'That's all right, dear,' she replied. 'You'll be out at work all day.'

223. Groom: 'Would you be very annoyed with me if I confess that all my upper teeth are false?'

Bride: 'Not at all, darling. At least I can now relax and take off my wig, inflatable bra, glass eye and artificial leg.'

224. The spry old gentleman of 89 had just returned from his honeymoon with his 23-year-old bride.

'How did the honeymoon go?' asked a friend.

'Oh, it went quite well,' replied the old man, 'but did you ever try to get a marshmallow into a kid's piggy bank?'

HORSES

225. 'How is your yearling coming along?' one gentleman asked another as they chatted in the Silver Ring at Ascot.

'It died,' said the other.

'That must have lost you a fortune, with the training fees and everything,' sympathized the first man.

'No, I made a profit actually,' the owner chuckled. 'I raffled him at £5 a ticket.'

'Didn't anyone sue you for fraud?'

'No. The winner got a bit shirty but I sent *him* his money back!'

226. Two thickies bought themselves a horse each and decided to keep them in the same field.

'How shall we tell which horse is which?' asked Paul.

'I'll tie a blue ribbon to the tail of my horse,' replied Rene.

Unfortunately, the ribbon on Paul's horse fell off one day in Paul's absence, so the two were again faced with the problem of deciding which horse was which.

'I know,' suggested Paul, 'you have the brown horse and I'll have the white one.'

HOSPITAL

227. Stockbroker patient: 'Tell me, nurse, what is my temperature?'

Nurse: 'A hundred and one.'

Stockbroker patient: 'When it gets to a hundred and two – sell.'

228. The pompous patient had annoyed everyone in the ward. The nurses were tired of his amorous advances at them, and the other patients had rapidly become irritated with his highly detailed boasts of his probably fictional conquests of numerous women.

One young nurse decided to teach the man a lesson.

'Now, sir, I want to take your temperature as the doctor instructed,' she explained. 'So I'll just close the screens around your bed and then you must take your pyjamas off.'

'Oh, ho, ho!' said the man, loudly. 'So you fancy a bit of slap and tickle with Mr. Fantastic himself, eh? Fancy asking me to take my pyjamas off just to take my temperature! A likely story!'

'I'm serious,' insisted the nurse. 'The doctor has ordered a rectal temperature to be taken.'

'You mean, you want to stick the thermometer up my . . .'

'Yes,' replied the nurse hastily.

Soon the screens were in position around the man's bed, his pyjamas were removed, and the nurse carried out her plan.

'There, I'll have to leave the thermometer in position for a few minutes,' said the nurse, and left the enclosure around the bed.

For the next five minutes the ward was filled with muffled giggles and shrieks of laughter.

'What's all the noise?' asked the matron, entering the ward and noticing a lot of nurses and patients peering in through gaps in the screen around the man.

On entering the enclosure around the man's bed, the matron demanded of the man: 'What is the reason for this?'

'For what?' asked the man. 'The nurse is taking my temperature.'

'With *this*?' demanded the matron, taking a tulip out of the man's behind to the accompaniment of riotous laughter from the onlookers who were still peering in through the screens.

229. Molly, one of the nurses in the hospital, was always going around joking and laughing and teasing the patients.

Knowing Molly's sense of fun, one of the male patients named John decided to play a little trick on her.

When asked to provide a specimen of his urine he took some orange squash which his mother had brought for him and poured this into the bottle instead.

When Molly came to collect the sample, John made as if to hand the bottle over to her – but then said:

60

'Hmm. It looks a bit weak. I'd better pass it through again.'

He then put the bottle to his lips and drank the contents. Molly fainted.

230. Nurse: 'Can I take your pulse?
Patient: 'Why? Haven't you got one of your own?'

231. The 'phone rings and matron answers the 'phone: 'Yes. Hello. You want to know how Mr. Gough is doing? His operation seemed to go extremely well and we have every hope that he can leave the hospital soon. Might I know who is speaking so I can pass on your interest and concern to him?'

The voice on the 'phone answers: 'This *is* Mr. Gough. They don't tell patients themselves *anything* in this place!'

232. There was a very high pitched scream from the operating theatre, and then the doctor's voice could be heard: 'Nurse! I said take off the patient's *spec*tacles.'

HOTELS
233. The young man arrived late at night at a small hotel in a remote village in Scotland.

After a hot supper, the middle-aged owners of the hotel bid him good night, but warned him: 'Make sure you lock your bedroom door before going to sleep as our Stella walks in her sleep.'

The young man, with visions of a delicious young female named Stella sleep-walking into his room, made sure to leave his door open.

Two hours after falling asleep he was rudely awakened by a coarse tongue licking his face and a heavy weight on his chest and body. He opened his eyes to see Stella, the biggest sheepdog he'd ever seen.

234. You can always tell if you're in a honeymoon hotel – all the couples start yawning at five in the afternoon.

235. Traveller: 'Excuse me, do you have a room for tonight?'

Hotel proprietor: 'Certainly, sir. It'll be fifteen pounds a night. Or I can let you have a room for only five pounds if you make your own bed.'

Traveller: 'I'll take the five pound room.'

Hotel proprietor: 'Right! I'll just go and fetch the wood, the hammer and the nails and other materials for the bed . . .'

236. Hotel receptionist in Spain to Englishman: 'Are you a foreigner?'

Englishman: 'Certainly not! I'm British!'

237. 'Are the sheets clean?' asked a tourist at a small hotel in New York.

'Of course they're clean,' snapped the manager. 'I washed them only yesterday. If you don't believe me you can feel them – they're still damp.'

238. The new porter at a hotel in Mexico had been given careful instructions as to how to behave with courtesy and efficiency.

'You should try and welcome each guest by name,' instructed the hotel manager.

'But how can I do that? How will I know their names?' asked the porter.

'Simple!' explained the manager. 'Each guest usually has his or her name written on their luggage.'

So the first couple to enter the hotel and be welcomed

by the new porter were greeted: 'Welcome, Mr. and Mrs. Simulated Real Leather.'

HOUSEKEEPER
239. Mabel is the best housekeeper in the world. She's been divorced fifteen times – and she's still got the house.

HOUSE-WARMING PARTY
240. 'Would you like to come to my house-warming party on Friday?'

'I'd love to! What's the address?'

'Number six, Labrador Crescent. Just ring the bell with your elbow.'

'Why can't I ring it with my finger?'

'You're not coming empty-handed, are you?'

HUSBANDS
241. My husband is a self-made man who loves his maker.

242. Janice: 'My husband tricked me into marrying him. Before we married he said he was a multi-millionaire.'

Berenice: 'He *is* a multi-millionaire, isn't he?'

Janice: 'Yes. But he also said he was eighty-one and in poor health – but I've just found out he's only eighty and in perfect condition.'

243. If my husband ever had any get-up-and-go it got up and went before I met him.

244. My husband is a very noisy eater. Last night we went to an exclusive, cosy little night club and when he drank his soup five couples got up to dance the cha-cha.

245. My husband is such a hypochondriac he refused to kiss me until I bought lipstick with penicillin in it.

246. You can always find my husband at a party, even if you've never met him before. All you have to do is find a situation where two people are talking – if one of them looks extremely bored, then it's my husband who's doing the talking.

247. My husband is a regular churchgoer – he never misses the Christmas Eve service.

248. My husband insists he's not bald – just that his hair is flesh-coloured.

249. My husband isn't exactly stupid – it's just that he's been educated beyond his intelligence.

250. My husband is so short-sighted he can't get to sleep unless he counts elephants.

251. My husband believes so devoutly in reincarnation his Will leaves everything to himself.

252. My husband is so thin and has such a gigantic nose and enormous ears that whenever he stands up in a restaurant people hang their coats and hats on him.

253. My husband keeps boasting to people at parties that he has more than a thousand people under him. So he does – he's a gardener in a cemetery.

254. My husband wanted to be a tree surgeon when he was young – but he couldn't stand the sight of sap.

255. My husband has got such a long face that his barber charges him double for shaving it.

256. My husband always drinks with a friend – that way he's got someone to carry him home.

257. My husband never gets a hangover – he's always drunk.

258. My husband isn't a hard drinker – he finds it very easy.

259. The only thing my husband ever achieved on his own is his moustache.

260. The reason my husband is so thin is because when he went to donate blood he forgot to say 'when'.

261. You can always tell when my husband has just told a joke at a party – the whole room goes deathly quiet.

I

INHERITED WEALTH
262. Claude was so wealthy that even the bags under his eyes had his initials on them.

263. The hereditary peer was boasting of his ancestors and generally acting in an arrogant and disdainful manner towards one of his fellow club members who was a self-made man.

Eventually, the man could stand the peer's attitude no longer and said, in a loud voice: 'From what you have been saying it would appear that the nobility of my family begins with me, whereas that of yours ended with your father.'

264. The extremely wealthy man (who had inherited his wealth) bought his son a slum. He wanted him to have everything he missed when he was a child.

265. The young man knew his aged aunt was extremely wealthy and dearly loved her poodles, so he visited her every day to take the dogs for walks in the hope of convincing his aunt that he was a suitable major beneficiary under her will.

A short time later the old lady died. She left him the poodles.

266. He's so wealthy he even bought a kid for his dog to play with.

INSURANCE AGENT
267. Insurance agent: 'Now, madam, this policy is a particularly good buy. Under it we pay up to five hundred pounds for broken arms or legs.'

Woman: 'But what do you do with them all?'

IRISH

268. The Irishman wanted to go surf riding – but he couldn't persuade the horse to go in the water.

269. Timothy was on holiday in Ireland and staying at a small country inn.

One evening in the bar he was amazed by the following conversation:

'That's a beautiful hat you've got there,' said an old man to a young fellow who was standing next to him at the bar. 'Where did you buy it?'

'At O'Grady's,' replied the young man.

'Why, I go there myself!' commented the old man. 'You must be from around these parts, then?'

'Aye. From Murphy Street.'

'Gracious!' exclaimed the old man. 'I live there, too!'

'Quite amazing,' commented Timothy to the barman, 'that those two folk over there live in the same street and have only just met.'

'Don't you believe it!' said the barman. 'They're actually father and son but they're always too drunk to recognize each other.'

270. Irishman: 'If God didn't want me to have any more children he wouldn't let me drink on Saturday nights.'

271. 'I bet you don't know how many sheep there are in this field?' said the English farmer to the Irish visitor.

The Irishman glanced around the field and then replied: 'Three hundred and eighty-six.'

The farmer was astonished. 'That's incredible! You're perfectly right. How did you manage it?'

'Oh, it was quite simple,' said the Irishman. 'I just counted the number of legs and divided by four.'

272. Shaun: 'What's in your bag?'
George: 'Chickens.'
Shaun: 'Will you give me one of them?'
George: 'No.'
Shaun: 'If I guess how many you've got in your bag, then will you give me one?'
George: 'Certainly! If you guess correctly I'll give you both.'
Shaun: 'Six.'

273. José was on holiday in Killarney and talking to Patrick.
'We have a word in Spanish,' he said, 'mañana. It means tomorrow – it will have to be tomorrow. It seems to be a difficult idea to translate. Do you have a word for it in your country?'
'No,' said Patrick, after a considerable pause for thought, 'I don't think we have any word with quite such a sense of urgency!'

274. An Irishman walks into a bar to find his friend chatting to the barman. Perched seductively alone at the other end of the bar is a stunning girl. So he says to the barman, 'Give me two whiskeys, have a drink for yourself, and let's have one for the gorgeous lady.'
Knowing his customer quite well the barman thought it was only fair to give him a word of warning. He whispered, 'I don't think you need bother sir – she's a lesbian.'
The Irishman thought about this for a minute but then insisted she be bought a drink. Later he wandered

over to say hello and said, 'Good evening; now tell me, and what part of Lesbia do you hail from?'

275. 'That will be £2.50, Paddy,' said the cashier of the car wash.

How did you know I was Irish?' asked the Irishman, paying the money.

'Easy,' replied the girl. 'We don't get many motorcyclists in here!'

276. The bright Irishman says he won't buy a nuclear fall-out shelter now, but will wait until he can buy a cheaper one second-hand.

277. Paddy was having dinner with some friends in their house in Donegal when a severe snow storm developed.

'You must stay the night with us,' insisted his friends. 'You can't possibly go home in this weather.'

'That's very civil of you,' replied Paddy. 'I'll just go home and bring my pyjamas.'

278. Why does an Irishman look in a mirror with his eyes closed? To try to see what he looks like when he's asleep.

J

JAPANESE

279. It was an international television conference in the USA and the delegates were eating the farewell dinner of the conference.

A Japanese gentleman was sitting next to a delegate from Portland, Oregon. After the Japanese had finished his soup, the American asked him 'Likee soupee?' The Japanese gentleman nodded.

Throughout the meal, the American asked such questions as: 'Likee fishee?' and 'Likee drinkee?'

When the meal was finished, the chairman of the conference rose to his feet and introduced the Japanese gentleman as the guest speaker of the meeting.

The Oriental gentleman gave a witty, excellent speech on the future of broadcasting – speaking in English much better than anything any American has ever uttered.

After his speech, the Japanese gentleman returned to his seat and asked his American table companion: 'Likee speechee?'

JEWISH

280. 'And how is your son?' asked Mrs. Goldberg.

'Oh, he is a constant joy to me,' replied Mrs. Cohen.

'But how is that possible? Surely you know he is homosexual?'

'Yes, I know,' agreed Mrs. Cohen, 'but recently he has been going out with such a nice Jewish lawyer.'

281. Did you know it was the Jews who were to blame

for the sinking of the Titanic? Well – Goldberg, Iceberg, what's the difference?

282. A mohel opened a shop and displayed some plastic dustbins in the window. (A mohel is the person who carries out the Jewish circumcision operation.)

Anyway, a man went into the shop and said: 'I'd like a plastic dustbin, please.'

The mohel replied: 'I'm afraid I don't sell them.'

'But you've got plastic dustbins in the window!' exclaimed the man.

'So?' shrugged the mohel, 'what would you have put in the window?'

283. 'Stand still!' rasped Ikey as he pointed the gun at the Postmaster, 'these bullets cost a lot of money!'

K

KNOCK, KNOCK
284. 'Knock, knock.'
     'Who's there?'
     'Machiavelli.'
     'Machiavelli who?'
     'Machiavelli nice suit for seventy pounds.'

L

LANGUAGES
285. Gum Arabic: spoken by Arabs without teeth.

LAW
286. Judge: 'Have you ever been up before me before?

Prisoner: 'I don't know, your honour. What time do you usually get up?'

287. The man stood in the dock, accused of raping a dog. The judge was passing sentence and said: 'This is the most disgusting case I have ever had to try. It's very difficult to think of a suitable sentence for you, but . . .'

The judge was interrupted by a voice from the back of the court yelling: 'Give him the cat!'

M

MOTHER-IN-LAW

288. My mother-in-law believes in free speech – particularly long-distance 'phone calls from our house.

289. For eleven years Duncan had put up with the fat, interfering old woman. Now he could stand it no longer.
'She's got to go,' he said to his wife. 'I can't stand your mother another minute!'
'My mother!' exclaimed Duncan's wife. 'I thought she was *your* mother!'

290. 'My mother-in-law has gone to the West Indies.'
'Jamaica?'
'No – she decided to go by herself.'

291. My mother-in-law is very spiteful. When she caught rabies she wrote down a list of people she wanted to bite.

292. They did things differently when my mother-in-law was a girl – otherwise they'd never have classified her as a girl.

293. 'My mother-in-law has gone to Indonesia.'
'Jakarta?'
'No – she went by 'plane.'

294. Fred: 'My mother-in-law arrived unexpectedly last night and since we were short of beds she had to sleep in the bath. But the stupid woman fell asleep and left the water running.'
Tom: 'Did the bath overflow?'
Fred: 'No. My mother-in-law always sleeps with her mouth open.'

MOUSE
295. When Mr. Mouse discovered his wife struggling helplessly in a bowl of water, he dragged her out and gave her mouse to mouse resuscitation.

N

NEWS

296. Reports are just coming in about a woman photographer in Clapham who committed suicide by drinking a bottle of varnish. She left a note saying she did it because she wanted a glossy finish.

297. On Wednesday, three Irishmen hi-jacked a submarine, and then demanded half a million pounds – and three parachutes.

298. A famous Australian jewel thief and homosexual was arrested in Sidney today.

299. On the business front, sales of tiaras increased enormously this afternoon – it was tiara boom today!

300. The latest thing in female clothing is men.

301. On Friday an Irishman tried to blow up the QE2, but had to give up when he couldn't get his mouth over the funnel.

302. Five people broke out of prison last night by stealing a lorry load of senna pods. It is believed the criminals are still on the run.

303. A politician was arrested today for impersonating a human being.

304. Police want a man of medium build and average height for assault on young women. Unfortunately, they didn't state what salary they were offering.

305. The latest fashion news from Paris is that skirts will remain the same length as last year – but legs will be shorter.

NIGHTCLUB
306. The nightclub dance floor was so crowded that one young girl fainted and had to finish the dance before she could fall down.

NOTICES
307. In a record shop there was a notice stating: 'Mendelssohn's Organ Works'. Underneath this notice someone had pinned a note on which was written: 'So does mine'.

OBITUARY COLUMNS
308. I always read the obituary columns every morning to see if I'm alive or dead.

309. My wife reads the obituary columns and thinks it very odd that people keep dying in alphabetical order.

OLD AGE
310. The grand old man at the Home was celebrating his 112th birthday and the reporter from the local newspaper asked him: 'Tell, me, what do you think is the reason for your long life?'

The old man thought for a moment, then said: 'Well, I suppose it's because I was born such a long time ago.'

P

PARTY

311. 'I say, old man,' said Clive to the host of the party, 'there's this rather delectable young chick whom I'm getting along really well with, if you know what I mean.' He winked, and continued: 'And I wondered if I might use your spare bedroom for a short while.'

'No, I don't mind,' replied the host, 'but what about your wife?'

'Oh, don't bother about her,' said Clive. 'I'll only be gone a short time and I'm sure she won't miss me.'

'I *know* she won't miss you,' stated the host, 'it's only five minutes ago that *she* borrowed the spare bedroom!'

312. It was a fancy dress party and the young girl said to the man: 'I'm supposed to be a turkey – what are you?'

'Sage and onions,' he replied.

PERSONNEL MANAGER

313. 'What can you do?' asked the Personnel Manager.

'Lots', replied the young man. 'I can play golf, talk a public school accent, make boring speeches, have affairs with secretaries without my wife finding out, go to sleep in the back of a Rolls Royce, and generally get publicity for working as hard as possible while in reality doing nothing at all.'

'Excellent,' said the Personnel Manager. 'You can start tomorrow as Managing Director.'

POET

314. The poet had been boring everyone at the party by

droning on and on about his various sources of inspiration and how/he was trying to compose a poem using trochaic dimeter brachycatalectic.

Towards the end of the party he approached a sweet young girl and said: 'You know, I'm currently collecting some of my better poems for an anthology to be published posthumously.'

'Oh good!' said the girl, with true feeling. 'I shall look forward to it!'

POLICE

315. Detective's assistant: 'Sir, I have found a box of vestas with your name on it.'

Detective: 'Ah! So at last I have met my match.'

316. The pretty young girl coming home by car late at night after visiting her boyfriend's house was stopped by a policeman and asked to take the breath test.

The girl blew into the breathalyzer and it instantly changed colour.

'Hmm,' said the policeman. 'You've had a stiff one tonight miss.'

'My God!' exclaimed the girl. 'Does that show, too?'

POST OFFICE

317. The little old lady went to the post office and handed over the counter a large parcel, on which she'd written 'Fragile' numerous times and in large letters.

Counter clerk: 'Is there anything breakable in this parcel?'

Little old lady: 'Of course not! "Fragile" simply means unbreakable in Latvian.'

PRESS REVIEWS

318. 'We hope the author will soon be needing our services' – *The Coffin Makers' Gazette*.

319. 'The writer of this book is a genius. By the way, I must thank him for such a fantastic weekend at his cottage in the country. This, of course, in no way influenced my opinion of his work.' – *A. Female-Critic*.

320.'This book is brilliant.' – *Daily Liar*.

321. 'He is certainly one of our best writers and will surely become as famous as William Shakespeare – the William Shakespeare of 112 Railway Arches, Neasden, Alaska.' – *Anony Mouse*.

PROVERBS

322. People who cough loudly never go to the doctor – they go to the cinema.

323. The more you understand the less you realize you know.

324. Laugh and the world laughs with you: weep and you sleep alone.

325. Every woman worries about the future until she has acquired a husband, whereas men never worry about the future until they get a wife.

326. Never tell a psychiatrist you're a schizophrenic. He'll charge you double.

327. Success doesn't always go to the head – more often it goes to the mouth.

328. Anyone who boasts about his ancestors is admitting that his family is better dead than alive.

329. The less people know, the more stubbornly they know it.

330. The first sign of old age is when you still chase girls but can't remember why.

331. If at first you don't succeed you're just like 99.99 per cent of the population.

332. You can always tell when politicians are lying – their lips move.

333. The best distance between two points is cleavage.

334. If it wasn't for venetian blinds it would be curtains for all of us.

335. Holidays in the USA make you feel good enough to return to work – and so poor that you're forced to.

336. The only thing you can be sure of getting on your birthday is a year older.

337. A hypochondriac's life is a bed of neuroses.

338. People who sleep like babies never have any.

339. One of the first signs of getting old is when your head makes dates your body can't keep.

340. The only way in Britain to make money go further is to post it overseas.

341. Absence makes the heart go wander.

342. Never try to make love in a field of corn. It goes against the grain.

343. It's not safe to drink and drive – you might stop suddenly and spill some of it.

PSYCHIATRIST

344. 'Please can you help my brother? He thinks he's a cat.'

'How long has he thought that?'

'Since he was a kitten.'

345. Q. 'What are the differences between psychologists, psychoanalysts and psychiatrists?'

A. 'Psychologists build castles in the air, psychoanalysts live in them and psychiatrists collect the rent!'

346. Some time ago a young man was committed by his family to a mental home. This greatly upset a wealthy friend of his, who immediately started spending a good deal of time and money to secure his release. After nearly two years of patient effort he succeeded in lining up three psychiatrists who testified that the young fellow was completely normal and always had been. The friend whisked the doctors and the ex-patient off to his flat for dinner and a celebration. Before the evening was over he asked, 'What are you going to do now? Go away for a holiday, I suppose, and then settle down as before.'

'Well, I thought of getting something to do, actually,' was the reply. 'Something quiet, of course, but interesting. Like writing a book. I have not really made up my mind whether to do that or take up painting again. On the other hand, of course, I might just go on being a tea-cosy.'

QUESTIONS

347. How do you get down from an elephant? You don't – you get down from a duck.

348. What is worse than when it's raining cats and dogs? When it's hailing taxis.

349. If it takes five men fifteen hours to build a brick wall, how long would it take ten men to build it? No time at all, because the five men have already built it.

350. Why do bees have sticky hair? Because they use honey combs.

351. Why can't a bicycle stand up? Because it's two-tyred.

352. What is the favourite food of hedgehogs? Prickled onions.

353. Which side is it best to have the handle of a teacup on? The outside.

354. Where was the Declaration of Independence signed? At the bottom.

355. What is furry, crunchy, and makes a noise when you pour milk on it? Mice crispies.

356. What is in Paris, is very tall, and wobbles? The Trifle Tower.

357. Do farmers take pig sties for grunted?

358. Have you heard the joke about quicksand? It takes a long time to sink in.

359. Do Arabs dance sheik to sheik?

360. What do you call a very large animal which keeps taking pills? A hippo-chondriac.

361. What did the policeman say to his stomach? I've got you under a vest.

362. What is black and white and red all over? A sunburnt zebra.

363. What tables can you eat? Vegetables.

364. What is above a Rear-Admiral? His hat.

365. Where does Friday come before Tuesday? In a dictionary.

366. Why do storks only lift one leg? Because if they lifted the other leg they'd fall over.

367. What do you get when you cross some grass seed with a cow? A lawn moo-er.

368. What do you do when your nose goes on strike? Picket.

369. What is wet, black, floats on water and shouts 'Knickers!'? Crude oil.

370. What is wet, black, floats on water and whispers 'Undergarments'? Refined oil.

371. Where do you take a sick horse? To a horse-pital.

372. What is the word with four letters, which ends with 'k' and is another word for 'intercourse'? Talk.

373. What do policemen eat for tea? Truncheon meat.

374. What was the first thing Henry III did on coming to the throne? He sat down.

375. What do you call a man who breaks into a house and steals ham? A ham burglar.

376. At what battle did Nelson die? His last one.

377. What wears a cowboy hat, holds two guns and lives under water? Billy the Squid.

378. Have you heard the story about the giant gate? You'll never get over it.

379. What do rich turtles wear? People-necked sweaters.

380. Why do moths fly with their legs so far apart? Did you ever see the size of a moth ball?

381. What is the last thing you take off before going to bed? Your feet off the floor.

382. How do you start a flea race? One, two, flea, go.

383. How do you catch homosexual mice? Use a pooffy cat.

R

RATS
384. 'Did you hear about Adam?' asked the brown rat.

'No. What happened?' said the black rat.

'He was feeling rather depressed and flushed himself down the toilet.'

'Oh!' said the black rat. 'He committed sewercide.'

RED INDIAN
385. The Red Indian who always suffered from colds was named Running Nose.

RELIGIOUS
386. Rabbi Cohen and Father O'Connor were at a party when they were each offered a ham sandwich.

Rabbi Cohen declined the sandwich, and the Catholic priest chided him: 'Come, come, rabbi – when are you going to become liberal enough to eat ham?'

The rabbi smiled and replied: 'At your wedding, Father O'Connor.'

387. Three Scotsmen were visiting London for a holiday and on Sunday they went to Church. As the collection plate moved closer and closer to their pew they became more and more worried.

Just before the plate reached them, one of the Scotsmen fainted and the other two carried him out of the Church.

388. Cynthia: 'What do you think of the new clergyman?'

Janice: 'Very good. I didn't know much about sin until he came.'

389. The rabbi and the priest lived next door to each other and bought new cars almost exactly at the same time.

Looking out of his window, the rabbi saw the priest with a small bowl of water sprinkling the contents over the car and blessing it.

Not to be outdone, the rabbi got a hacksaw and cut half an inch off the exhaust pipe of his own car.

390. One clergyman had a flashing orange nose so he was known as a Belisha Deacon.

RESTAURANTS

391. Customer: 'Why is this chop so terribly tough?'
    Waiter: 'Because, sir, it's a karate chop.'

392. Customer: 'Excuse me, but how long have you been working here?'
    Waitress: 'About three months, sir.'
    Customer: 'Oh. Then it couldn't have been you who took my order.'

393. 'Waiter! There's a fly in my soup.'
    'Would you prefer it to be served separately?'

394. 'Waiter! There's a fly in my soup.'
    'If you throw it a pea it'll play water polo.'

395. 'Waiter! There's a fly in my soup.'
    'No sir, that's the chef. The last customer was a witch doctor.'

396. 'Waiter! There's a fly in my soup.'
   'If you leave it there the goldfish will eat it.'

397. 'Waiter! There's a fly in my soup.'
   'I know, sir! It's fly soup.'

398. 'Waiter! There's fly in my soup.'
   'Oh, dear, it must have committed insecticide.'

399. 'Waiter! There's a fly in my soup.'
   'I'm sorry, sir, the dog must have missed it.'

400. 'Waiter! There's a fly in my soup.'
   'That's the meat, sir.'

401. 'Waiter! There's a fly in my soup.'
   'It's the rotting meat that attracts them, sir.'

402. 'Waiter! How dare you splash soup on my trousers!'
   'I'm sorry sir, but now you've got soup in your fly.'

403. An American tourist, visiting England, had just enjoyed a delicious dinner in a Winchester restaurant.
   'Would you like coffee, sir?' inquired a waiter.
   'Certainly,' replied the American.
   'Cream or milk?'
   'Neither,' said the American, firmly. 'Just give me what I'm used to back home: a pasteurized blend of water, corn syrup solids, vegetable oil, sodium caseinate, carrageenan, guargum, disodium phosphate, polysorbate 60, sorbitan monostearate, potassium sorbate and artifical colour.'

404. Waiter: 'What would you like, sir?'
   Customer: 'Steak and chips.'
   Waiter: 'Would you like anything with it, sir?'
   Customer: 'If it's like the last one I ate here, then bring me a hammer and chisel.'

405. Customer: 'Have you got asparagus?'

Waiter: 'No, we don't serve sparrows and my name is *not* Gus.'

406. 'Waiter! Please bring me a coffee without cream.'

'I'm very sorry, madam, but we've run out of cream. Would you like it without milk instead?'

407. Waiter: 'Would you like something to eat?'

Customer who has waited forty-five minutes for service: 'No, thank you – I don't want to waste my lunch hour.'

408. The loud-mouthed American from Mobile, Alabama, was in the coffee shop of an expensive hotel in London.

'How would you like your coffee, sir?' inquired a waiter.

'I like my coffee just like my women – strong and sweet,' replied the American.

'Quite, sir,' said the waiter. 'Black or white?'

RETIREMENT

409. The couple had just reached retirement age, but Mr. Robinson was a very worried man.

'We don't really have enough to live on,' he confessed to his wife. 'Sure, our pension is enough to survive – but we lack sufficient savings to give us a few extra pleasures like the occasional evening at the cinema or a decent holiday once a year.'

'Don't worry,' replied Mrs. Robinson. 'I've managed to save a few thousand pounds.'

'However did you manage that?'

'Well,' said Mrs. Robinson, a bit shyly, 'every time

you made love to me these past thirty years I've put fifty pence in my own bank account.'

'But why did you keep it a secret all these years?' demanded Mr. Robinson. 'If I'd known about it I'd have given you all my business.'

ROMANCE

410. Bill can read his girlfriend like a book – in bed.

411. 1st girl: 'What would you give a man who has everything?'

2nd girl: 'Encouragement.'

412. Girl: 'I'll pour the drinks, dear. What will you have – gin and platonic?'

Young man: 'I was hoping for whisky and sofa.'

413. Paul: 'Is it true you proposed to that awful Gruntswick woman at the party last night?'

David: 'Unfortunately, yes.'

Paul: 'And she accepted your proposal. But didn't you only meet her at the party?'

David: 'Yes. But after five or six dances together I couldn't think of anything else to talk about.'

414. It was breakfast one month after their marriage.

'Darling,' said the wife. 'Will you love me when I'm old and wrinkled.'

The husband lowered his morning newspaper and said: 'Of course I do.'

415. 'Susan has been married and divorced so many times to wealthy men she must be getting richer by decrees.'

416. 'My dearest, sweetest, beautiful darling! Will you love me always?'

'Of course, darling. Which way do you want to try first?'

417. Man: 'What would I have to give you to get a little kiss?'

Girl: 'Chloroform.'

418. The young man asked the beautiful young girl to marry him, pointing out that his father was 103 years old and that he was heir to his father's substantial fortune.

The girl asked the young man for time to consider his offer and, two weeks later, she became his step-mother.

419. Dashing young Edward was walking through the park one afternoon when he heard a female voice cry out: 'Get down, you beast! If you put your filthy paws on me once more I'll never come on the grass again.'

He rushed behind the hedge from whence the voice had come, hoping to rescue a fair maiden from a foul creep – but instead discovered a little old lady talking to her pet dog.

420. 'Darling, you have the face of a saint.'

'Dearest, you say the sweetest things! Which saint?'

'A Saint Bernard!'

421. A man of thirty was talking to his girlfriend. 'I've been asked to get married hundreds of times,' he said.

'Oh!' replied his girlfriend, rather astonished. 'Who by?'

'My parents,' he replied.

422. After going into Hazel Wood with his girlfriend, a

disappointed Fred came out and wrote under the sign which said 'Hazel Wood' the words: 'but Janice wouldn't'.

423. 'Sir, I'd very much like to marry your daughter,' said young Wilkins, a junior clerk in the Company in which his prospective bride's father was the Personnel Officer.

'I see,' replied the man. 'Write out your qualifications, name, address and any other details you think appropriate and leave it with me. If no other suitable applicants turn up then I'll ask you to come for a further interview.'

424. Young man: 'Oh, my gorgeous, sweetest darling! Am I the first man you've ever been to bed with?'

Young girl: 'Of course you are! Why do all you men always ask the same stupid question?'

425. Cuthbert: 'Darling, if we get married do you think you will be able to live on my income?'

Ethel: 'Of course, darling. But what are *you* going to live on?'

426. My girlfriend rejected me because she said she liked the little things in life – a little house in the country, a little yacht, a little multi-millionaire . . .

427. Glennis: 'I hear Diana is getting married next week.'

Jenny: 'Is she pregnant?'

Glennis: 'No.'

Jenny: 'I'm not surprised – I always knew she was a snob.'

428. David saw a beautiful young girl walking along the

beach, dressed in an extremely tight pair of denim shorts which emphasized every movement of her walk.

Being a daring sort of fellow, he went up to the young girl and said: 'I'm sorry to trouble you – but I'm fascinated about your shorts. How can anyone possibly manage to get inside such a tight garment?'

The beautiful young girl smiled and replied: 'You can start by asking me out to dinner.'

429. The eighty-nine year old man confided to his best friend that he was pinning all his hopes on being a late developer.

430. Ethel: 'Dearest, will you still love me when my hair has all gone grey?'

Richard: 'Of course, dear. If I loved you when your hair was blonde then brunette then black then red – why should grey make any difference?'

431. Although she was only the architect's daughter, she let the borough surveyor.

432. My girlfriend has an hour-glass figure, but gets a bit annoyed if I put my arms around quarter to nine.

433. 'I've just become engaged,' said Sally, flashing her ring around the typing pool.

'Yes,' said one of her colleagues, Kathy. 'The person who gave it to you is about six feet tall, has medium length brown hair, blue eyes, and a small tattoo in the shape of a butterfly on his right shoulder.'

'Fantastic, Sherlock Holmes!' exclaimed Sally. 'You can tell all that just by looking at the ring?'

'Certainly,' replied Kathy. 'It's the one I gave him back six months ago.'

434. It was in a nudist camp and the beautiful young woman walked over to the young man.

'Pleased to meet you,' said the man.

The girl looked down, blushed, and said: 'I can see you are.'

435. Adrian: 'Why do all the men find Victoria so attractive?'

Simon: 'Because of her speech impediment.'

Adrian: 'Her speech impediment?'

Simon: 'Yes. She can't say "no".'

436. My girlfriend was arrested in one of those conservative foreign countries for wearing a bikini top that was far too small, even though the policeman who arrested her agreed with me that she had two fantastic excuses.

437. An extremely attractive young girl rushed into a pub and demanded a drink.

'How old are you?' asked the publican.

'Sixteen,' replied the girl.

'Then you've had it,' replied the publican.

'I know,' panted the girl. *'That's* what made me so thirsty.'

438. 'Will you kiss me?'

'But I have scruples.'

'That's all right. I've been vaccinated.'

439. Young girl: 'Stop!'

Young man: 'No.'

Young girl: 'Well, at least I resisted.'

440. Dennis knew he was really getting places with his girlfriend, Carol, when she invited him around to her parents' house, saying: 'We can have a great time

together, I'm sure, as my parents are going to a concert and will be out the whole evening.'

Thus, on the great day he stopped in at a chemist's shop on his way to his girlfriend's house. The chemist was such a friendly man that Dennis found himself confiding to him about how beautiful Carol was and how he hoped she would appreciate his thoughtfulness in coming prepared with some contraceptives.

When Dennis arrived at Carol's house he found her waiting for her father to come home from work, while Carol's mother was beautifying herself ready for the concert.

As soon as Carol's father arrived home, Dennis suddenly became very agitated and kept stammering and suggested, loudly: 'C . . . Carol, I . . . I . . . th . . . think we should j . . . join your p . . . parents and go to the c . . . c . . . concert tonight.'

'Oh!' said Carol, disappointedly. 'I didn't know you liked classical music, Dennis.'

'I don't,' hissed Dennis. 'But then, I didn't know your father was a chemist!'

441. 'Whisper those three little words that will make me walk on air.'

'Go hang yourself.'

442. 'Er . . . um . . . excuse me for troubling you, but would you agree to come out with me tonight?'

'I'm sorry, but I never go out with perfect strangers.'

'Who said I was perfect?'

443. 'My girlfriend says I'm handsome.'

'That's only because you feed her guide dog.'

444. John could marry any girl he pleased – trouble is, he didn't please any of them.

445. When I first went out with my girlfriend she made me lay all my cards on the table – Barclaycard, American Express . . .

446. The beautiful young girl was walking along the street when a young man walked up beside her and said: 'Hello, beautiful! Haven't we met somewhere before?'

The girl gave him a frosty stare and continued walking.

'Huh!' snorted the young man. 'Now I realize my mistake – I thought you were my mother.'

'That's impossible,' retorted the girl, 'I'm married.'

447. 'That man's annoying me.'
'Why? He's not even looking at you.'
'I know. *That's* what's annoying me!'

448. Mavis fell in love with her boyfriend at second sight – the first time she didn't know he had any money.

449. 'Is it true you've fallen in love with Dracula?'
'Yes. It was love at first bite.'
'My! How fangtastic!'

450. I went out with a female spiritualist last night – I wanted to try a new medium.

451. Man: 'Have you been to bed with anyone?'
Girl (angrily): 'That's my business!'
Man: 'Oh! I didn't know you were a professional.'

452. Peter received the following letter from his girlfriend:
'Darling Peter,
    I'm so sorry I quarrelled with you and called off our

wedding. I'm terribly, terribly sorry for all the hateful and spiteful things I said about you and do hope you will forgive me. Whatever you want of me I shall try to give – and do hope you will give me one more chance. I know I said I was leaving you for Tony, saying he was a much better man than you, but I never honestly meant it. Tony means nothing to me. You are the only one in my heart. You, Peter, are all that I desire. Please forgive me and take me back,

Your ever-loving Janice.

P.S.: May I take this opportunity to congratulate you on winning such a large amount on Premium Bonds.'

453. Young man: 'If you argue with me just once more I shall kiss you passionately all over.'

Girl: 'No you won't.'

454. Young girl: 'Darling, do you think I should wear my short green Chinese silk dress or my long fawn woollen dress tonight?'

Young man: 'I don't mind what you wear, dearest. You know I'll love you through thick or thin.'

455. 'How was your first date with John?'

'Oh, it was all right until after dinner. But on the way home he stopped the car in a lonely lane and started kissing me and generally distracting my attention. He then started feeling my bra and around my panties – but I fooled him. I'd hidden my money in my shoe . . .'

456. My girlfriend told me last night that she really loved me. But I think it's only puppy love as she was panting, licking my face, and rubbing me behind the ears at the time.

457. 'Dolly, I've got some fantastic news for you,' said

Samantha to her sister. 'My boyfriend has finally persuaded me to say "yes".'

'Fantastic!' replied Dolly. 'Congratulations. When will the wedding be?'

'Wedding? Who said anything about a wedding?'

458. Fred is extremely broadminded – he's got nothing else on his mind.

459. Betty: 'Is it true your boyfriend is an identical twin?'

Clare: 'Yes.'

Betty: 'But don't you have difficulty telling them apart.'

Clare: 'No. His sister's got a moustache.'

460. 'Where did you get such lovely red hair?'

'From standing on my head such a lot – the blood stains it red.'

461. His girlfriend is such a snob she won't eat hot dogs unless they've been registered at the Kennel Club.

462. It had been a very enjoyable party and David, a young man with a Texan drawl, appeared to get on very well with a pretty young English girl named Sally – although both had met each other for the first time at the party.

'Can I see you home?' inquired David.

Sally reached into her handbag and produced a photograph of her house.

463. Young man: 'Do you think you could be happy with a man like me?'

Young girl: 'Of course! So long as he wasn't *too* much like you.'

464. Claudia refuses to go out with married men – she insists they come in to her flat!

465. 'I love you much, much more than anyone else in the whole wide world.'

'You mean, you've had them all, too?'

466. Young girl: 'Darling, will you love me when I get old?'

Young man: 'Of course I'll love you. Our love will grow stronger with each passing hour. Our love will endure throughout eternity. But you won't be looking like your mother, will you?'

467. 'I'll give you just fifteen minutes to stop doing that . . .'

468. The couple were on a pre-honeymoon cruise when suddenly a storm blew up and their ship was smashed to pieces by the powerful waves.

Clinging to a plank of wood, the couple managed to survive in the sea for two days without food or water.

On the third day, the man began to pray even more frantically than before: 'Oh, dear Lord, please save us. Please – we beg you to spare our lives and make us safe and end our misery in this cruel sea. Please – if you save us I promise to give up the sins of gambling, smoking, swearing, drinking, and I will refrain from . . .'

He was interrupted by his girlfriend, who said: 'Better stop there – I think we're approaching land!'

469. An old gentleman asked the pretty girl if she wanted to come up to his room to help him write his will.

470. David had asked Mr. Cohen if he could marry his daughter, and Mr. Cohen was now considering the matter.

'Would you still love my Rebecca as much if she was poor?' he asked.

'Of course, sir!' replied David, with feeling.

'Then you can't marry her,' said Mr. Cohen. 'I don't want a fool in the family.'

471. Barry's girlfriend refused to marry him because of religious differences – he was poor and she worshipped money.

472. Mabel and Arthur had been living together for thirty-five years as man-and-wife.

One day Mabel was reading a romantic women's magazine when she suddenly looked up at Arthur and said: 'Why don't we get married?'

'Don't be crazy,' replied Arthur. 'Who would want to marry us at our time of life?'

473. His girlfriend is so thin it takes three of her to make a shadow. Once when she swallowed a prune she was rushed to the maternity clinic.

474. 'Oh, Brian, Mum wouldn't like it.'

'Your mother isn't going to get it!'

475. David and Debbie both worked in the same office in Hong Kong, and both of them were Chinese.

For more than six months David had admired Debbie from a distance, never managing to pluck up sufficient courage to ask her for a date, but all the time his passion for her grew stronger and stronger.

At last the great day came when he somehow managed to scrawl a note to her asking if she'd like to have dinner at a restaurant with him.

'I'd love dinner with you,' she replied, coming over to his desk in their open-plan office to tell him so in person, and making him blush with pleasure.

That evening in the restaurant he asked her what she would like to eat, and she studied the menu carefully, then said: 'I'll have shark's fin soup, please. And Peking duck with dumplings, some suckling pig, steamed fish, and then some fresh lychees.'

David was horrified, as he'd been mentally calculating the enormous cost of all this food – the most expensive items on the menu and more suitable for a wedding feast than for a dinner for two.

'D . . . D . . . do you eat like this at home?' he stammered, his face blushing red again.

'No,' replied Debbie. 'But then, no one at home desperately wants to go to bed with me.'

476. 'The manager of our office gave me a mink coat for Christmas.'

'To keep you warm in winter?'

'No. To keep me quiet.'

477. Pretty young girl: 'What are we going to do today?'

Young man: 'How about a drive in the country?'

Pretty young girl: 'Will there be any kissing and cuddling and parking in lonely lanes and all that sort of thing?'

Young man: 'Certainly not!'

Pretty young girl: 'Then what are we going for?'

478. Young man to attractive young girl: 'I'd like to see you in a two-piece outfit – slippers!'

RUSSIAN

479. The Russian chauffeur was driving the Chief American Attaché through the Moscow streets to an important Kremlin meeting.

'There is the tallest building in Moscow,' he told the Attaché, pointing to the Lubianka.

The 'Top Brass' American, knowing that this quite low building was the HQ of the KGB, was puzzled but thinking he did not wish to look stupid, said nothing.

Later, on the way back, his Russian driver, who was a man of few words, repeated the same thing. The American this time was too intrigued to keep quiet and asked him what he meant by saying this was the tallest building in Moscow, when so many others around were obviously higher.

'Oh,' smirked the Russian, 'it is because in there, even from the dungeons, you can see all the way to Siberia!'

S

SADIST
480. A sadist is someone who would put a drawing-pin on an electric chair.

SCHOOL
481. Religious knowledge teacher: 'Now, children, I've just described all the pleasures of Heaven. Hands up all those who want to go there?'

All the children put their hands up, except for Debbie.

Religious knowledge teacher: 'Debbie, why don't you want to go to Heaven?'

Debbie (tearfully): 'I'd like to go, miss, but me mum said I had to come straight home after school.'

482. The little girl was accused of cheating during the biology examination – the teacher found her counting her breasts.

483. School teacher: 'Can you stand on your head?'
Pupil: 'No. I can't get my feet up high enough.'

484. Teacher: 'Susan, give me a sentence beginning with "I".'
'Susan: 'I is . . .'
Teacher (angrily): 'Susan! How many more times do I have to tell you! You must *always* say "I am"!'
Susan: 'All right, miss. I am the letter in the alphabet after H.'

485. Little Simon was the school swot – the other kids used to pick him up and bash flies with him.

486. Woman: 'Tell me, Des, how do you like school?'

Des: 'Closed.'

487. 'Hello,' said the school teacher, answering the 'phone. 'This is Miss Engels of Form Two of Mudleigh Junior School.'

'Hello,' said the voice on the 'phone. 'I'm 'phoning to tell you that Jim Brown is sick and won't be coming to school today.'

'Oh, I *am* sorry to hear that,' commented the teacher. 'Who is that speaking?'

The voice on the telephone replied: 'This is my father.'

488. Teacher: 'Now, James, if you bought fifty doughnuts for one pound, what would each one be?'

James: 'Stale, miss! They'd have to be, at that price.'

489. Teacher: 'Wendy, can you put "defeat", "deduct", "defence", and "detail" in a sentence?'

Wendy: 'Yes, miss. De feet of de duck gets under de fence before de tail.'

490. Teacher: 'Now, Susan, can you tell me where God lives?'

Susan: 'Miss, I think he lives in the bathroom.'

Teacher: 'In the bathroom! Why do you think that?'

Susan: 'Because every morning I can hear my father knock on the bathroom door and say: "God, are you still in there?" '

491. Teacher: 'What is the difference between the death rate in Victorian England and the present day?'

Pupil: 'It's the same, sir. One per person.'

492. Religious knowledge teacher: 'Now, Timothy, where do naughty boys and girls go?'

Timothy: 'Behind the bicycle shed in the playground.'

493. The two little girls were talking at school during playtime.

'Do you know how old teacher is?' asked Janice.

'No,' replied Sybil, 'but I know how to find out.'

'Oh, how?'

'Take off her knickers.'

'Take off her knickers!' exclaimed Janice. 'How will *that* tell us.'

'Well, in my knickers it says "4 to 6 years".'

SCOTTISH

494. The rich old Scotswoman of few words discovered that her husband had died during the night. She wondered for a moment how to break the news below stairs. Then she rang her bell for the maid who arrived breathlessly within a trice.

'Josephine,' instructed the thrifty old bird, 'you need only boil *one* egg for breakfast!'

495. The Englishman was in a restaurant in Scotland when he was suddenly attacked by a severe burst of coughing and sneezing – and he sneezed so violently that his false teeth flew out of his mouth and dropped to the floor, where they broke at the feet of a Scotsman.

'Don't worry, sir,' said the Scotsman. 'My brother will soon get you a new pair and at far less cost than an English dentist would charge. And he can provide a suitable set almost immediately.'

The Englishman couldn't believe his luck and gladly accepted the Scotsman's offer.

The Scotsman left the restaurant and returned nine minutes later with a pair of false teeth which he handed to the Englishman.

'Fantastic!' exclaimed the Englishman, trying the teeth. 'They fit perfectly. Your brother must be a very clever dentist.'

'Oh, he's not a dentist,' replied the Scotsman. 'He's an undertaker.'

496. Did you hear about the Scotsman who died of a broken heart? He was tired of reading jokes about how mean the Scots are so he went into his nearest pub and ordered a round for everyone.

'That's very kind of you, sir,' commented the barman. 'There's almost fifty people in here. I didn't know you Jews were so generous.'

497. A Scotsman was carrying a large bottle of whisky home when he tripped on the stairs to his house and fell heavily.

Feeling a horrible wetness come over his hands he couldn't bear to look down for fear it was the whisky rather than blood.

498. A Scottish couple went to a restaurant in London and each of them ordered a steak.

The waiter was surprised to see the woman eating while the man merely looked at his plate without eating.

'Is there something wrong with your meal, sir?' asked the waiter.

'Oh, no!' replied the man. 'It's just that my wife is using the dentures first.'

499. The Scotsman was visiting London for the day and called upon a lady of pleasure in Soho and, after he had partaken of her bodily delights, he gave her two hundred pounds.

'Why, that's incredibly generous of you!' exclaimed the surprised lady. 'No man has ever before given me so much. And yet, from your accent you sound Scottish, which makes it even more incredible for you to be generous. Which part of Scotland do you come from?'

'From Edinburgh,' replied the Scotsman.

'How fantastic! My father works in Edinburgh.'

'I know,' said the Scotsman. 'When your father heard I was coming to London he gave me two hundred pounds to give to you.'

500. The difference between a Scotsman and an Englishman can easily be discovered by letting loose a cow in their front gardens.

An Englishman will wail to his wife: 'Come quick and help me get rid of this horrible cow that's eating my prize lawn!'

The Scotsman will call to his wife: 'Come quick and bring a bucket – there's a cow on the lawn and it wants milking.'

501. The shy English girl on her first visit to Scotland nervously went up to a handsome young Scot who was wearing his national costume and asked: 'Excuse me speaking to a stranger, but I've always been curious. Please can you tell me what is worn under the kilt?'

The Scotsman smiled and said: 'Nothing is worn – everything is in excellent condition.'

SECRETARIES

502. Secretary: 'Please, Mr. Jenkins, can I have two weeks off work?'

Mr. Jenkins: 'What for?'

Secretary: 'I'm getting married.'

Mr. Jenkins: 'But you've only just returned from

your three week summer holiday! Why didn't you get married then?'

Secretary: 'What? And ruin my summer holiday?'

503. Personnel Manager: 'How well can you type?'

Young secretary: 'My typing isn't very good – but I can erase at sixty-five words per minute!'

504. Fred: 'My secretary is a biblical secretary.'

John: 'A biblical secretary? What's that?'

Fred: 'One who believes in filing things according to the Bible saying: "seek and ye shall find".'

505. Personnel Manager: 'Can you do shorthand?'

Young secretary: 'Yes. But it takes me longer.'

506. The angry employer was berating his sweet young secretary: 'Who told you that you could have the morning off just to go shopping? And now you have the cheek to ask for a salary increase – merely because you came with me as my assistant to the conference in Brussels last weekend! Who gives you encouragement for such fantastic ideas?'

Secretary: 'My legal adviser, sir.'

507. The boss leaned over his secretary, who was busily painting her fingernails, and said: 'Miss Ruggles, I'd like to compliment you on your work – but when are you going to do any?'

508. Mavis: 'On the way to work this morning a man stopped me in the street and showed me the lining of his raincoat.'

Claudia: 'Are you sure he only wanted you to see his raincoat?'

Mavis: 'Oh, yes! He wasn't wearing anything else.'

509. Mrs. Jones: 'I'm Mr. Jones's wife.'

Beautiful young secretary: 'Are you? I'm his secretary.'

Mrs. Jones: '*Were* you?'

510. My secretary is called 'Good Time' – because she's the good time that's been had by all.

511. Senior civil servant: 'Did you 'phone my wife as I asked you to?'

Secretary: 'Certainly, sir. I told her you would be late home from the office due to an unexpected conference.'

Senior civil servant: 'And what did she say?'

Secretary: 'Can I rely on that?'

512. Secretary to an irate gentleman on the 'phone: 'Oh! Didn't you get our letter – I'm about to post it now.'

513. His secretary is a miracle worker – it's a miracle if she works.

514. One boss had to fire eleven secretaries because of mistakes they wouldn't make.

515. His secretary thinks she's clever. She's joined as many unions as possible so she gets more chances of being called out on strike.

516. The sweet young secretary is busy applying make-up when the 'phone rings. She picks up the 'phone and a voice says: 'Is Mr. Schwartz in yet?'

'No,' replies the secretary, 'he hasn't even been in yesterday yet.'

517. My secretary has only been working for me for two weeks and already she's a month behind.

SEX

518. The slightly worried parents inquired of their son how the lesson on sex went that day. They were hoping that the teacher had not been too 'progressive'.

The boy gave a somewhat bored reply: 'Oh,' he said, 'it was useless – we only had the theory today!'

SHAKESPEARE

519. One day William Shakespeare was finding it difficult to concentrate on his writing work. Inspiration seemed to have deserted him.

Then, as he sat gnawing his pencil he glanced at it and suddenly creative thoughts rushed into his head and he began to write: '2B or not 2B . ₂ .'

SHOPPING

520. Customer: 'Please do you have a dress that would match the colour of my eyes?'

Honest salesgirl: 'I'm sorry, madam, but they don't make material in bloodshot.'

521. Tailor: 'Your suit will be ready in six weeks, sir.'

Customer: 'Six weeks! But God made the whole world in only six days!'

Tailor: 'Quite true, sir. But look what state the world is in.'

522. A man bought a bath and was just leaving the shop with his purchase when the shop assistant called: 'Do you want a plug?'

'Why?' asked the man. 'Is it electric?'

523. 'Do you sell dogs meat?'

'Certainly – if they come here with their owner.'

524. A shopkeeper was held up by a man waving a

bunch of flowers at him in a threatening manner. It was robbery with violets.

525. Retired Army colonel: 'I'd like some pepper, my good man.'

Shop assistant: 'Certainly, sir! What sort would you like – white pepper or black pepper?'

Retired Army colonel: 'Neither. I want toilet pepper!

526. After searching all over the department store's furnishing section, a woman sighed: 'They don't make antiques like they used to do!'

527. 'Is this a second-hand shop?'

'Yes.'

'Please can you fit one on my alarm clock?'

528. The lift in the large department store was extremely crowded, and as the lift attendant closed the doors he called: 'Which floors, please?'

A young man standing near the back of the lift cried out: 'Ballroom!'

'Oh, I'm sorry,' said a large lady in front of him, 'I didn't know I was crushing you that much.'

SONGS FOR FISH AND ANIMALS

529. 'Mackerel The Knife.'

530. 'My Bear Lady.'

531. 'I've Got Ewe Under My Skin.'

532. 'Snake, Rattle And Mole.'

533. 'Weasel Overcome.'

534. 'Tie A Yellow Gibbon Round An Old Oak Tree.'

535. 'Whale Meat Again.'

536. 'Jack The Kipper.'

537. 'I'm Gonna Wash That Man Right Out Of My Bear.'

538. 'Hit The Road Yak.'

539. 'If You Were The Only Gill In The World.'

540. 'Red Snails In The Sunset.'

541. 'Amazing Plaice.'

542. 'Salmon Chanted Evening.'

543. Fly Me To Baboon.'

544. 'What Kind Of Mule Am I?'

SOUP

545. Cannibal: 'What kind of soup is this?'
'Bean Soup' said the waitress.
'Human Beings?' queried the cannibal.

SPIES

546. The aspiring spy was being interviewed in Whitehall by a Secret Service Chief, who was explaining the sort of men he looked for.

'We need people who are more than just involved,' he said. 'In this game you have to be committed. It is rather like the difference between bacon and eggs. So far as the chicken is concerned with the production of this marvellous start to the day – well she *is* involved; but the pig, *he* is committed!'

STATISTICIAN

547. A statistician is a person who, if you've got your feet in the oven and your head in the refrigerator, will tell you that, on average, you're very comfortable.

T

TAXI DRIVERS

548. An Englishwoman and her young son were travelling in a taxi in New York, USA.

As the taxi passed a particularly seedy part of the city, the small boy was fascinated by the garishly made-up ladies who were walking along the streets accosting some of the male passersby.

'What are those ladies doing?' asked the boy.

His mother blushed and said, somewhat embarrassed: 'I expect they are lost and are asking people for directions.'

The taxi driver overheard this, and said in a loud voice: 'Why don'tcha tell the boy the truth – in udda woids they're prostitutes.'

The woman blushed even deeper red, and her son asked: 'What are p ... p ... pros ... what the driver said? Are they like other women? Do they have children?'

'Of course,' replied his mother. 'That's where New York taxi drivers come from.'

TEACHER

549. The teacher wanted to find out who was responsible for a suspicious pool of water near the blackboard. She instructed all her children to shut their eyes so that whoever it was could step forward and write his or her name on the blackboard.

Everyone, including the teacher, closed their eyes tightly and presently a telltale tip-toeing could be heard approaching the board. After a few nasty squeaks with the chalk the tip-toe could be heard padding back.

When everyone opened their eyes, *another* pool of water had appeared – and on the blackboard was written 'The phantom widdler strikes again!'

TELEPHONE
550. 'Why don't you answer the 'phone?'
    'Because it's not ringing.'
    'Why must you leave everything until the last minute?'
551. Over the 'phone some voices are very difficult to extinguish.

TELEVISION
552. Please do not turn off your brain. A normal society will be resumed as soon as possible.

TIME
553. It's easy to make time fly: just throw an alarm clock over your shoulder.

TIPSTER
554. Buried deeply in his Form book and with the television blaring the young husband absentmindedly looked over at his bouncing baby boy playing on the floor and mentioned to his wife, 'Baby's nose is running again.' 'Can't you think of anything but horses!' she snapped.
555. So there was this racing tipster handing out *free* tips. 'No need to pay unless you win sir!' he chortled, as he worked through the long queue – handing each punter a slip with a different horse named on it.

U

USA
556. The largest women in the USA are Mrs. Sippy and Miss Oury.

USSR
557. In the USSR all the history books have loose-leaves.

558. Russian soldiers always patrol in threes. This is because one is able to read, one is able to write, and the third is there to stop these two intellectuals from becoming capitalists.

W

WATCH
559. 'I've got an amazing watch. It only cost me fifty pence.'

'Why is it so amazing?'

'Because every time I look at it I'm amazed it's still working.'

560. What goes 'tick, tock, woof'? A watch dog.

WEATHER
561. The hard pressed managing director had just returned from a gruelling overseas trip and was relaxing at home when the telephone rang. When he hung up almost at once his wife inquired who it was.

'Someone with the wrong number my love,' he said. 'He wanted to know if the coast was clear. So I suggested he telephone the Met. Office!'

WEDDING
562. The woman wearing an enormous flowery hat was stopped at the entrance to the church by one of the ushers.

'Are you a friend of the bride?' asked the usher.

'Of course not!' snapped the woman. 'I'm the groom's mother.'

WEDDING PRESENTS
563. My brother is so mean. Before I got married he promised us a food mixer as a wedding present, and I was so surprised at his unexpected generosity. On the

wedding day, however, he handed me his carefully wrapped food mixer – a wooden spoon!

564. It was the woman's second marriage and her first husband was kind enough to send the happy couple a wedding gift of a carving set – two chisels and a hammer.

WEDDING RECEPTION

565. 'Psst!' said the slimy looking man to the groom. 'Do you have any photos of your wife in the nude?'

'Of course not!' growled the groom.

'Want to buy some?' asked the slimy looking man.

566. The happy couple proudly displayed all their wedding gifts at the reception – including an envelope from the groom's father marked 'Cheque for five hundred pounds'.

'Who is that strange man pointing at your father's cheque and laughing?' asked the bride.

The groom looked at the offending person, blushed, and said: 'My father's bank manager.'

567. The bride had got a little drunk and was having some difficulty in making her speech of thanks for all the wonderful wedding gifts.

At the end of her speech she pointed rather unsteadily towards an electric coffee percolator, and said: 'And, finally, I'd like to thank my husband's parents for giving me such a lovely perky copulator.'

WEIGHING MACHINE

568. Jack's wife stepped on the weighing machine which also produced a fortune reading on the other side of the weight indicator card.

Out popped the card, and Jack's wife said: 'It says I'm attractive, have a pleasing personality and can charm anyone I meet.'

'Huh!' muttered Jack, taking the card from his wife. 'Even the weight is wrong!'

WIVES

569. Fred: 'My wife converted me to religion.'

Bill: 'Your wife converted you to religion? How did she do that?'

Fred: 'Because I didn't believe in Hell until I married her!'

570. Jim is terribly sad. His wife has run off with his best friend – and he misses his friend terribly.

571. 'What's the trouble? You look really miserable.'

'It's Fiona, your wife.'

'My wife?'

'Yes. I'm afraid she's been unfaithful to both of us.'

572. I call my wife a wonder woman – I sometimes wonder if she's a woman.

573. I've got the most sexy, witty, creative, intelligent wife in the world ... I just hope her husband doesn't know about it.

574. 'I hear your first two wives died of mushroom poisoning. And now you tell me your third wife, has just died as a result of falling off a cliff. A bit strange, isn't it?'

'Not really. She refused to eat the poisoned mushrooms.'

575. Farmer's wife: 'I'm thinking of divorcing Joe.'

Mabel: 'But why?'

Farmer's wife: 'Because he smokes in bed.'

Mabel: 'Surely that's not sufficient reason? Only smoking in bed?'

Farmer's wife: 'Ah! But Joe smokes bacon.'

576. After spending a fortune on my wife for beauty treatments I can honestly say that the only thing that makes her look good is distance.

577. My wife is so jealous that when she couldn't find any female hairs on my coat she accused me of going out with bald-headed women.

578. Tom: 'There's one word that describes my wife: temperamental.'

John: 'In what way?'

Tom: 'She's fifty per cent temper and fifty per cent mental!'

579. I wouldn't say my wife had a big mouth, but she called me from London yesterday. I was in South-ampton at the time and we don't *have* a telephone!

580. It's not that my wife was fat when I married her – it's just that when I carried her over the threshold I had to make two trips.

581. Joe got a letter from his wife today. It read: 'Dear Joe, I missed you yesterday. Please come home as soon as possible and let me have another shot.'

582. My wife isn't exactly fat and ugly, but whenever she goes to the doctor he tells her to open her mouth and say 'Moo!'

583. There's nothing wrong with his wife that a good funeral wouldn't cure.

584. Cuthbert's wife made him a millionaire. Before he married her he was a multi-millionaire.

585. My wife is so fat if she was a stripper she'd have to wear a G-rope.

586. Adrian was, as usual, complaining about his wife. 'She's always breaking her promises,' he said. 'Before we married she claimed she'd die for me – but she hasn't.'

587. Bill: 'I think a wife of forty should be like pound notes.'
  Tom: 'In what way?'
  Bill: 'You could change a wife of forty for two twenties.'

588. 'Why do you call your wife Camera? Surely that's not her proper name?'
  'Her real name is Gladys – but I call her Camera because she's always snapping at me.'

589. My wife has a photographic mind – but it's a great pity it never developed.

590. When Fred's wife was born they fired twenty-one guns. Unfortunately, they all missed.

591. My wife is so ugly whenever she goes to the zoo she has to buy two tickets – one to get in, and one to get out.

592. Clive: 'I can find my wife anywhere I go?'
  Robert: 'How?'
  Clive. 'All I have to do is open my wallet – and there she is.'

593. A month ago my wife put mud all over her face to improve her looks. It improved them so much she hasn't taken the mud off yet.

594. My wife had plastic surgery last week – I cut off her credit card.

595. Clive: 'Tony, is it true you married Cynthia for the money her grandfather left her?'

Tony: 'Of course not! I would still have married her if someone else had left her the money.'

596. My wife takes three hours to eat a plate of alphabet soup – she insists on eating it alphabetically.

597. 'My wife is an Eighth Day Adventist.'

'Don't you mean a 7th Day Adventist?'

'No – she's always late for everything.'

598. My wife is so stupid she once took a tape measure to bed with her to try and discover how long she slept.

599. My wife has a better sense of judgment than I have – she chose me as her husband.

600. My wife insists she's not fat – just that she's three feet too short for her body.

601. 'I didn't make love to my wife before we were married. Didn't believe in that sort of thing. Did you?'

'Don't know. What did you say your wife's name was?'

602. 'Where did you get such a nice suit?'

'It was a present from my wife. I came home unexpectedly early from the office the other evening, and there it was – hanging over the back of a chair in the bedroom.'

603. John: 'My wife's a kleptomaniac.'

Richard: 'Is she taking anything for it?'

604. The best years of my wife's life were the twenty between eighteen and twenty-nine.

605. As a wedding anniversary gift, Frank Smith bought his wife one of those recorded message machines that record telephone calls when you are out. The first day she got it she fitted it up to say: 'This is the Smith residence. Unfortunately, Mrs. Smith is out but this machine will record your message. Please start your rumour or gossip now . . .'

606. My wife is the only person I know who can ruin cornflakes – she boils them in the packet.

607. My wife is so conceited she only looks at me because she can see her own reflection in my spectacles.

608. Whenever I argue with my wife we soon patch things up – like my black eye, my broken nose, broken arm . . .

609. My wife is so stupid she went window shopping the other day – and came home with five windows.

610. My wife is so fat that whenever she takes a shower her legs don't get wet.

WRITER

611. Writer: 'I took up writing full-time about a year ago.'

Friend: 'Have you sold anything?'

Writer: 'Yes – my colour TV, all the furniture, the carpets, the house . . .'

Z

ZEBRAS

612. Farmer Giles went to the sales to buy himself a horse. Unfortunately that day there were no horses but the final lot to come up was a zebra and even though he knew that no one had ever trained a zebra to do anything before, he decided to make a low offer. Naturally he got it. Knowing what he knew he immediately told the zebra that when he got back to the farm he was to go around all the animals and chat to them about their work and then decide what he could do best. He warned the zebra that if he did not become a useful animal within six weeks he would be packed off to the abattoir.

So the zebra lost no time in talking to the animals. He asked the hen first, what did she do? 'Oh well,' cackled the hen, 'I peck around in the farmyard here, pick up a few worms and as long as I lay an egg every day old Giles leaves me alone – it's a good life really.' 'I don't think I would like that,' said the zebra, 'I think I will go and talk to the pig and see what he does.'

He explained to the pig the stern command that he had had from Giles and asked him what he did. 'Oh, I enjoy myself,' the pig snorted, 'I snuffle around in this mud and he gives me lots of hot potato peelings and good food and doesn't ask me for much. The only thing that worries me is that a few of my brothers have disappeared recently and I don't think what happens to them is terribly good news. Still, I live in the hope that my turn is yet a long way off.'

The zebra thought this was a little uncertain for him so he continued with his inquiries by asking the bull what he did for a living. The bull snorted impatiently, 'If you take those silly pyjamas off,' he roared, 'I will show you!'

ZOO

613. The little boy on his first visit to the zoo followed all the signs. He saw the sign which said 'To the Elephants' and enjoyed watching them, then followed the sign 'To the Penguins' and found their antics amusing; but when he followed the sign 'To the Exit' he was disappointed at finding himself back in the street outside the zoo without seeing the Exit animal.

OUR PUBLISHING POLICY

HOW WE CHOOSE

Our policy is to consider every deserving manuscript and we can give special editorial help where an author is an authority on his subject but an inexperienced writer. We are rigorously selective in the choice of books we publish. We set the highest standards of editorial quality and accuracy. This means that a *Paperfront* is easy to understand and delightful to read. Where illustrations are necessary to convey points of detail, these are drawn up by a subject specialist artist from our panel.

HOW WE KEEP PRICES LOW

We aim for the big seller. This enables us to order enormous print runs and achieve the lowest price for you. Unfortunately, this means that you will not find in the *Paperfront* list any titles on obscure subjects of minority interest only. These could not be printed in large enough quantities to be sold for the low price at which we offer this series.

We sell almost all our *Paperfronts* at the same unit price. This saves a lot of fiddling about in our clerical departments and helps us to give you world-beating value. Under this system, the longer titles are offered at a price which we believe to be unmatched by any publisher in the world.

OUR DISTRIBUTION SYSTEM

Because of the competitive price, and the rapid turnover, *Paperfronts* are possibly the most profitable line a bookseller can handle. They are stocked by the best bookshops all over the world. It may be that your bookseller has run out of stock of a particular title. If so, he can order more from us at any time we have a fine reputation for "same day" despatch, and we supply any order, however small (even a single copy), to any bookseller who has an account with us. We prefer you to buy from your bookseller, as this reminds him of the strong underlying public demand for *Paperfronts*. Members of the public who live in remote places, or who are housebound, or whose local bookseller is unco-operative, can order direct from us by post.

FREE

If you would like an up-to-date list of all the paperfront titles currently available, send a stamped self-addressed envelope to
ELLIOT RIGHT WAY BOOKS, BRIGHTON RD.,
LOWER KINGSWOOD, SURREY, U.K.